THOUGHT CATALOG BOOKS

Let's Agree to Disagree

Let's Agree to Disagree

13 Civil Dialogues On The Culture Wars

THOUGHT CATALOG

THOUGHT CATALOG BOOKS

Brooklyn, NY

THOUGHT CATALOG BOOKS

Copyright © 2016 by The Thought & Expression Co.

All rights reserved. Published by Thought Catalog Books, a division of The Thought & Expression Co., Williamsburg, Brooklyn. Founded in 2010, Thought Catalog is a website and imprint dedicated to your ideas and stories. We publish fiction and non-fiction from emerging and established writers across all genres. For general information and submissions: manuscripts@thoughtcatalog.com.

First edition, 2016

ISBN 978-1530747092

10 9 8 7 6 5 4 3 2 1

Cover design by © KJ Parish

Contents

Preface

Dialogue is a deliberate endeavor and one that we encounter daily: A discussion with a significant other about a vacation destination. A disagreement with a coworker about the best way to make a project more efficient. A debate with friends about which restaurant to choose for dinner. Dialogue is simply part of being a human who interacts with other humans. The stakes of dialogue are raised, however, when we have to think about them in the context of political, cultural, and economic institutions that govern us, especially in the midst of culture wars.

"Culture war" refers to the ideological conflict between groups and individuals in society. I would go further and describe it as the ongoing philosophical struggle over rights, privileges, power, identity, and space. It manifests itself in our conversations on race, gender and sex, sexuality, religion, politics and government, interpersonal relationships, the workplace, etc.

In the last decade, we have recurringly heard that the state of civil dialogue in the United States is failing and falling fast.

When I was in graduate school (2012 – 2015) studying Organizational and Multicultural Communication, I recall one professor commenting that many who had been in politics for decades, who had proverbially "seen it all," think the times that we are currently in are the worst they've seen in regard to dialogue in the public space.

Starting in the spring of 2015, part of my role at Thought Catalog as Senior Writer & Cultural Advocate was to engage commentators, thinkers, activists, writers, artists, and lay individuals in "cultural dialogues." The fundamental principle that guided my work was seeking and showcasing perspectives.

In these dialogues, I was not looking for or expecting "objectivity," an aim that I think many people in media and academic spaces – the spaces I am most familiar with – often assume should guide such cultural interactions. In fact, I approached these dialogues with an acceptance that I, like my guests, had individual experiences, biases, prejudices, and objectives in the way we approached different subject matters. While seeking truth is always the cultural observer's task, soliciting perspectives is also a necessary task that is arguably only narrowly secondary to attempting truth.

Let's Agree to Disagree is a collection of dialogues that discuss contentious issues such as race and identity, police brutality, and cultural appropriation, as well as comedy, dating, and sex, among other subjects. The topics were chosen based on news, cultural happenings, access to individuals, and personal interest. It is in many ways an imperfect collection and one that includes the sometimes immediate or incomplete or partially constructed viewpoints that may occur when exchange takes place between people. But these imperfections are also what makes this specific collection charming and raw and real.

I hope you find these dialogues educational and entertaining. But above all, I hope they encourage you, the reader, to participate in dialogue in a manner that is civil and fruitful. It is my hope that by talking and listening – which is how dialogue functions – we can approach our culture wars differently, even if sometimes all we might be able to do is agree to disagree.

Sincerely,

Kovie Biakolo

1

Is Multiculturalism For Everyone?

On March 22 2015, Jeremy Sheeler, a writer and video editor, wrote an article titled, "'Conservatives' Are The True Multiculturalists." Given my graduate study in multiculturalism, Sheeler proposed I read it. From an informal e-mail exchange, we then decided to formalize our exchange on multiculturalism and our different interpretations of its implications on individuals and groups in society.

Kovie Biakolo: Jeremy, I read your piece on multiculturalism last week. It was an interesting viewpoint, to say the least. I disagreed with it in parts – on an academic level, as well as coming from the perspective of certain political assumptions and definition of terms. So I want to start right at the very beginning. In front of a general audience, whose political leanings and perspectives you are unaware of, how do you *simply* define multiculturalism?

Jeremy Sheeler: Hi, Kovie. Thanks so much for inviting me to this dialogue about such an important and timely topic. I think the best way I would define multiculturalism – in relation to the point I was trying to make in my piece and my general socio-political goals – is with the very broad definition I used in my piece: "Simply, the recognition that the world consists of many unique cultures, and the accompanying belief that there is value in this diversity" – that there is an inherent value in *diversity*.

KB: I agree wholeheartedly that there is a value to diversity and that multiculturalism necessitates a recognition of plurality of culture. I would add, however, that as a school of thought and a philosophical principle, multiculturalism is also included as a response to historical power being in the hands of particular bodies – notably white, Western, heterosexual men. And this response is involved in dismantling historical power in different spaces and institutions – from economics to narrative of self. But I do not agree with the notion that doing so creates a space in which multiculturalism negates the culture of those who have been historically in power. Practically speaking in terms of power dynamics, currently, that is not even possible.

So how, then, are conservatives who represent to some extent a preservation of this historical power considered the "true" multiculturalists?

JS: Multiculturalism as a "movement" is unequivocally spearheaded and perpetuated by Liberals – or, more accurately, Progressives. However, there is a deep contradiction between the political goals that these people claim to have and how their policies actually function. As I stated in my piece, Liberalism is premised upon universals – things that are true for all human beings, regardless of time, place, history, race, ethnicity, etc; or like in the language of the Declaration of Independence, "All [humans] are created equal." These principles are trans-cultural meaning they are not dependent on the accidents or vagaries of individual cultures, but true for humans, as such. What I mean when I say that "conservatives" are the true multiculturalists is that without certain individuals being willing to spurn universal values in favor of the particular ones based on the accidents of history, everyone will eventually believe and do the same thing: i.e. Liberalism. I mean "conservatives" as a category of worldview, not American Conservatives specifically.

KB: While accepting even in my own academic experiences that multiculturalism is more identifiable with the political left or "Progressive," I still disagree that it is exclusive to that political leaning because, while we are not here to talk about my politics, I am admittedly someone who is not left or right, obviously taking into consideration that I'm not even American at all. And I don't think I am exceptional. I do tend to believe, as Orwell so aptly acclaimed, that "all issues are political issues."

However, I think that there is a big problem in trying to essentialize people into one political ideology or perspective or belief. Most people, I think, are more complex than that, even when the political systems fail to allow them to participate in a way that represents their complex views. That aside, I also dissent from the belief that history is an accident; it cannot be if we create it every day in the way we tell stories about power and the past. And I would argue fundamentally that multiculturalism is ultimately a social conversation about *how* to deal with diversity in different spaces without being *ahisotrical*; a conversation that we all participate in, even unintentionally, whether we accept particular political ideologies or not.

Do you see how there might be a divisiveness in claiming that any one group authentically preaches multiculturalism or authentically practices it?

<u>JS:</u> I absolutely agree that people's actual worldviews do not fit nice and neatly into categories, a fact that is the main impetus for my writing. I think the media artificially divides us – but so has academia, the source of the ideas that the general culture now uses to discuss these issues. My piece was more about the theory than the individuals who hold them, though. People hold all sorts of contradictory beliefs at the same time – out of the necessity that the real world never actually conforms to the theories. But all I was trying to say was that without "conservatives" – i.e. those who conserve the particular beliefs of their ancestors and relatives – then there will be no diversity. Progressivism/Liberalism, though, is all about being an individual, about deciding things for yourself based on what you believe is the most authentic path for you, about autonomy.

It actively encourages people to break away from identity politics, so how can it also be the bulwark that preserves it?

KB: I will admit that my knowledge of political theory is not as current as it should be, considering it was my secondary subject of interest in college. But despite that shortcoming, it is my understanding that the conversation about autonomy and the role it plays of the individual, from Plato to Locke to Hobbes, has never been a certain one. And that is always my point in these sorts of ideological stances – we are always changing how we talk about these things as much as we change what we talk about when we talk about individual contracts to community. Identity politics, to those who are in bodies of historical power, may appear to contradict one's autonomy. But for those who are from communities that have been in positions of disadvantage, at the expense of those in historical power, their autonomy as individuals, like their community, use(d) identity politics as a way to counter their disadvantaged positions in the global space for their community as well as for their individual interests. This is to say, the two are not mutually exclusive. I do, however, want to ask:

Given that theory is different from practice, outside of multiculturalism and identity politics, how does one practice diversity and equality outside of multiculturalism in the nation-state and globe as we know it?

JS: Putting the disputes of theory aside, the problem I see with the paradigm of multiculturalism as practiced today is that it has made it impossible for people to create an identity. For white people (white Liberals), "we" hold that being an individual, having a mind of one's own, is the best way to be, whereas we think that "minorities" should be part of a community.

This is incredibly problematic for everyone involved, though. A) This notion of radical individuality/autonomy that we are supposed to aspire to, I would say, is "unnatural" – i.e. debilitating to our self and community; but B) it enchains minorities to identities/histories that they may not want to be associated with – i.e. when an African-American is accused of "acting white." "Acting white" simply means being autonomous, being liberated from identity politics.

As far as practicing diversity outside of multiculturalism, I think all one can do is recognize the limitedness of our perspective and be open to the Truth, wherever it may come from. The problem, though, is multiculturalism as proposed today denies us the right to make judgments about truth and falsity which ultimately just makes us indifferent to everything.

<u>KB:</u> I strongly reject the perspective that identity cannot be created in the current multiculturalism perspectives. Like all philosophical causes or movements, there are multiple ways to "do" multiculturalism. For all individuals, identity is not created in a vacuum, and for many individuals, especially those with histories that are not embedded in global power, identity construction occurring in multiculturalism has been more empowering than the alternative – which is identity construction according to historically prejudiced spaces. Even the example you give, "acting white" in the case of an African American or any black person, is based on constitutions of what "Whiteness" represents and doesn't and what "Blackness" represents and doesn't, especially in American society.

Thus even that statement is riddled in a history and context of prejudice.

I also find it difficult to accept that any philosophy denies the individual the practice to make their own autonomous judgments on worldview. If we need a big example, we might consider how feminism is hotly debated, especially in its third-wave by self-proclaimed feminists, and how it attempts to be individualized.

Indifference seems like the road we take far too often when the ideas become too complex, and these ideas are complex. But I would rather deal with that difficulty than the alternative of entirely doing away with a philosophical ideology that aims to be inclusive.

JS: "Acting white" can mean two different things, basically because of the push and pull of Western history and politics since the Enlightenment. There is the white "bourgeois" – for lack of better term – that has either merely gone along with or actively participated in the oppression you spoke of earlier; but then there are also Liberals/Progressives where "acting white" means being autonomous. The one I see most loudly proclaiming the value of multiculturalism, though, is the latter group. But this means autonomy for them, conformity for the others. While I understand the historical necessity of solidarity in group identity, until we figure out how to reconcile the incompatibility of solidarity and autonomy, then I feel like the whole thing is nothing more than a dog and pony show and everyone knows it. That's pretty much the entire premise of the television show *Community*: the incoherence and hypocrisy of the way it has been instituted and the way it papers over these tensions.

This was what I was trying to get at with my other recent piece, "Why White People Appropriate Black Culture." We are no longer having a real conversation about these issues because the words have lost all connection to reality. All we do is talk now.

KB: In the first place, I think the reconciliation between solidarity and autonomy is funny enough, culturally dependent on time and space. I have lived in societies that are more communal than individual, and vice-versa; the conversation of the compatibility between solidarity and autonomy is a human one that *ought* to change as what we know about the world, and who is in the world, changes.

With regard to conversations about reality and how we talk about cultural sharing, cultural exchange, and cultural appropriation, what I observe is, on the one hand, a struggle to define the terms. And then on the other hand is a struggle for power between groups, particularly historically disadvantaged groups wanting to correct what they see as wrongs of history versus historically advantaged groups wanting to maintain power for what I often deem as less complication for their individual and communal interests. Language and reality have always, I think, rested on each other. I don't think that there is a connection lost but rather a proliferation of voices in dialogue which makes the conversation more difficult. Again, that is not, to me, a bad thing but one that, now more than ever, the conversation needs to be approached with prudence by individuals and communities alike.

I am wrestling in particular with cultural appropriation versus exchange and participation, and I will probably write something about this soon. But as a way to end this dialogue, I want to specifically know the following:

Is it possible in American society, and given your viewpoint of multiculturalism and culture, for white people who have historically been in power here to participate in Black culture, without appropriating, whitewashing, essentializing it, etc.?

<u>JS:</u> That's exactly the problem, as I see it: it is *not* possible using those terms of critique. White people are in an impossible place today. We want to atone, but there is no way to do so. If we try to be post-racial, we are ignoring its complexity; if we we try to respect it, we are essentializing or stereotyping; if we try to emulate it out of true admiration, we are appropriating it. These "Cultural Marxist" critiques have made resolution impossible.

The only way I see us being able to get beyond this is to have a truly honest conversation about what it means to be a human being, to talk openly and honestly about the human condition, and to learn better ways of dealing with it. That, to me, is what culture is: a collection of wisdom about the best way to navigate the minefield of existence. "Multiculturalism," though, ossifies us into "dead" identities – ones that no longer match the world we are living in or approaching. I believe we need to all come together as Americans and forge a new identity that learns from the "best that has been thought and said in the world." This is an uncomfortable conversation, but I believe it is the only way we can ever reconcile the contradictions that we have created we reconsider all these recent incoherent theories.

KB: You know, I do think about and even empathize with the difficulty of navigating culture in general. In the context of a white person doing so in black American culture in an intentional manner, it isn't easy. What I think often goes unrecognized is that black Americans, like all people of color in this country, have had to navigate and negotiate their identities and participation in *(white) American culture* since the inception of this country, and we are still doing so today.

I think that multiculturalism is useful when its interpretations are utilized in a sense that firstly does appreciate the reality that you and I do live in different worlds, metaphorically speaking of course. We do see things differently. Our histories and our past and how we negotiate everything from identity to culture do not inherently match simply because we are both living, breathing, human beings. Coming together as a nation, as you suggest, will mean coming together with *Americans* who have a different history and experience and perception of not only the United States but of the world than you do, and many whose identities have to be negotiated with histories that are separate from *your* America.

Moreover, I think it would be intellectual narcissism to not see multiculturalism as something that is bigger than the American imagination of the world. Those narratives and experiences are important to the overall conversation as well. These conversations are uncomfortable for everyone, but they recognize that power and past play their roles. And I think it creates further problems when those in power police who and what is constituted in identity conversations within a culture. In the end, I think, context always matters. And the conversation must continue.

Thank you for being willing to have the conversation Jeremy – we need more of these.

JS: Actually, I think the main problem today is that we no longer are able to separate theory and context. Before we judge the accuracy of a statement, we must know all the relevant demographic information of the speaker – before we even begin thinking about whether what they say is *true*. Very likely, everything I've said today will be written off simply because I am a cis-gender, straight, white male. This type of atmosphere is completely anathema to not only academic and intellectual honesty but to simply being honest with yourself about who you are.

I'm not saying that context should not be considered but rather that it must be secondary to any pursuit of a viable means of moving forward together. The context adds too much passion and indignation into the mix for us to be honest with each other.

Thanks again, Kovie, for inviting me to have this dialogue today. I sincerely hope that it spurs many more of the kind and that one day we can all find a way to come together and fix our broken country.

After original publication of each dialogue, readers were welcomed to formally contribute to dialogues via email, indicating their commentary was for publication consideration. Reader Jason Koh, who is a political theorist, had the following commentary added to the dialogue.

Jason Koh: While I agree with certain portions of Jeremy's argument with regards to the contradictions that occur between the goals of multiculturalism and the ideological framework of traditional Liberalism, I feel as if Jeremy's critique is limited to one aspect of a larger problem concerning how we interact with the "other" (people of difference). He certainly does well to point out the problems of Liberalism in its attempts to unite various conflicting cultures under sterilized images palatable to Western Enlightenment thought.

But the view that multiculturalism finds its greatest affinity with Conservatism due to Conservatism's prejudicial aspects that attempt to preserve individual cultures through cultural antagonisms is what I find theoretically problematic. In the very same vein that Liberalism categorizes minority cultures to fit within its own ideological framework (as Jeremy talked about with regards to labeling minorities under identity politics), Conservatism frames other cultures under its own categorizations that fit within the narratives favorable to the traditions, myths and etc of the dominant culture within the cultural hegemony.

Whereas the goals of the two ideologies are different, they function along the same lines of conceptually removing the question of the "other." This is in the sense that one attempts to sterilize difference by assimilating and categorizing the pluralistic elements of culture under a unifying ideology and the other outright rejects or ignores the "other" in accordance to the ideological frameworks set by the dominant culture. As such, I feel as if to say that multiculturalism finds the greatest affinity towards Conservatism due the reactionary prejudices that aggressively acts to preserve certain cultural identities makes for a limited argument in my view.

2

Getting To Know The Redneck Who Hates White Supremacy

On April 2015, one Dixon D. White made a video on YouTube titled, "I'm a Redneck and I love America." The video went viral. In the video, Dixon discussed his perspectives on race and racism in the United States and why he advocates for racial healing as a self-proclaimed "redneck." I reached out to him to further discuss his views and the cultural implications of his video.

Kovie Biakolo: Hi, Dixon. Firstly can you tell us a little about yourself, why you identify as a "redneck," and what you're trying to do with the creation of your videos on white supremacy? What specifically and broadly led you to this journey?

Dixon D. White: I'm a country guy from a small town in Tennessee. I ride 4 wheelers and love my truck. I'm trying to start a movement of racial healing by reaching out to white

America and asking them to address our culture of white supremacy. As a group, white folks have never really dealt with our culture of white supremacy. But it's time for healing, and it's time to wake up out of denial. We need a national group therapy session that will lead us out of this insidious narcissistic disease.

What led me to this journey is suffering. Enduring and suffering emotional abuse as a child and then later on. When I was 18 and 19 in college, I was bullied and persecuted my freshman year. I had a low self-esteem and I think a lot of people took advantage of that. When I was 20, I finally began to understand why I had been abused a majority of my life. And it was because of prejudice and bigotry. Particularly elitism and the mentality of elitism was the reason for the abuse throughout my life. The kind of elitism I'm referring to is about supremacy in all its many forms. You have to be supreme and elite in every facet of yourself and life.

The prejudice I learned at 20 led me to take an oath with myself and with God that I would no longer be programmed by my environment and that I would always fight against prejudice and bigotry no matter what. That is what led me to listening to people of color which led me to the path of anti-racism.

KB: Some people would say that calling yourself a redneck is somewhat of a classist and even racist or prejudiced title. What's your response to that? And going further, some might argue that the redneck persona is an act. How do people know it's not?

DW: Well it's certainly not racist. It's a term, however ignorant, that is looked upon with affection in certain circles in the South. It's not politically correct, but it is effective in getting across my message. And I always have seen myself as a redneck or a country guy.

In the context of race, the term redneck has powerful connotations because it was the Southern culture that has always been the most overtly racist. When folks see a redneck speak the truth about our culture and system of white supremacy, they are shocked because of it's rarity. This is the reason that I believe this video has resonated with over 10 million people in 11 days.

As for it being an act, no, it's not an act because every single thing that I have said has come directly from my heart, and it's all completely true. I really do record my videos from my Ford F150 and I actually listen to country music regularly.

KB: How have your relationships changed in your personal and/or professional life since you've taken this stance?

DW: Well, about 11 days ago, my life was flipped upside down when my video went viral. Now I have interviews after interviews trying to get at me and reach me constantly. My social media is completely insane with love and support from everyone. Well, not everyone; but because of that, I have created a movement where I'm asking everybody to take a video racial healing challenge. I'm using whatever opportunities come my way to find a platform to make this movement happen. So far, people all over social media are posting videos about their experience and thoughts on our culture of white supremacy.

Since I became an anti-racist and started living my life in that way, I have lost many friends and have fought many people in my family. The good thing is I have also managed to reach people in my family and help them understand issues about race. I lost a really important job one time when I was younger fighting country racists. It was a really ugly scene in a factory that I worked in, and I regularly got death threats. Eventually, I was fired for standing up against these racists which led to me going into poverty for about three years. But it was well worth it, and I would do the same thing again if it came up.

KB: In your video, you talk about colorblindness and how a lot of white people like to use that as a reason for claiming they're not racist. Why, in your opinion, do (some) white people have such a hard time acknowledging color, and in general, seeing racism, even when people of color constantly are affected by it in their everyday lives?

DW: Colorblindness is a comfortable way of not having to face the reality that people of color live in. There is a grand ole tradition in America of protecting this great resource for white folks called white supremacy. White people have been indoctrinated and programmed by our white supremacist culture and environment to be apathetic, to be complacent, to be silent, to be dismissive, and to be eternally lost in denial when it comes to facing the simple reality of what we are doing to people of color. The key that white people have to learn is to let go of the fear and greed that keeps them firmly lost in the three Ds of racism – denial, defense, and delusion. I call this W.A.R.P. which stands for White American Racial Psychosis. This is the disease that I'm trying to fight.

KB: Do you think it's easier for white people to believe other white people's perspectives on racism? Doesn't that show a certain kind of white privilege, too? In some ways, do you think that in your case, you can be perceived negatively by some people as a "White Savior?"

DW: If there's one thing that I'd like everyone to remember that I've said, it is this: I have done and said nothing that people of color have not been saying for 400 years. It is exactly because of white privilege as to why their voices fall on deaf ears and why my voice is heard with enthusiasm and received so spectacularly. I have done nothing to deserve all this attention. I am only doing what all white people should do which is speak the truth, racially. However, I will take this attention and try to use it to build a platform for racial healing. As white people we've made this mess called white supremacy, and as white people, we have a responsibility to fix it.

Somebody once called me Redneck MLK, and to me, that's a horrific statement. Firstly, I am not a person of color. I don't live under the hell that people of color have to live under because of our racist institutions, systems, and culture. Secondly, the idea of being a White Savior is insanity to me. The only people who I'm lecturing to is the white community. I would never pretend to know what to tell the black community to do. It's not our place as white people.

KB: You seem to talk of race in a black/white binary context which is typical of how we talk about race in this country. But isn't that a problem, as well? It does tend to alienate other people of color from the conversation. What do you think about this, and how do we have better conversations about race in this country?

DW: That's why I often use the term "people of color" rather than just black or brown. In America, the darker your skin tone, the more hell you tend to catch. So I often mention brown and black when I'm referring to race because they tend to catch the most hell. In the conversations of race, you are correct. It is often limited to that black/white dynamic, racially. That's unfortunate because one of the greatest atrocities committed in America was against the indigenous people of the Americas, Native Americans. This is a conversation that needs to be discussed at least equal to the black/white discussion.

My father is Cuban and I've recently learned more about my Hispanic background at 48 years old. I've learned that there are many dynamics that are involved racially with Hispanics/Latinos. Many Latinos will deny that their brown or black skin has come from black people due to slavery in their country. White supremacy is worldwide and there are many areas and regions that need to be explored and discussed regarding race. I tend to focus on what I know as a Southern American.

I focus on my own white community with regards to addressing the problem that we created called white supremacy. It's up to people of color to discuss colorism and racism amongst themselves. I don't feel like it's my place to lecture people of color on what they need to do, racially.

KB: Finally, what do you want to accomplish with these videos and what do you think you will accomplish? In the near and distant future, what do you see happening in American culture in terms of how we deal with white supremacy and racism? Are we going to heal? Are we going to evolve? Will racism just always be around and our best bet is to reduce it the best we can in each generation?

DW: White folks in America, when it comes to race, are the most ignorant. It only benefits them and therefore blinds them to the realities of white supremacy's destructive power and structure in regards as to how it applies to people of color. My goal and my mission is to bring that uncomfortable reality into the hearts and minds of the white community by hoping that we can start a national conversation on race through social, viral videos.

When you have cancer, you have to identify it and come up with a plan to destroy it. It is exactly the same thing with racism. It has to be addressed, and it can never be ignored or swept under the carpet. We have to hit it straight on, bluntly, with full force. If our species can do that, then there is hope for true equality and justice for all. And as a species, if we cannot, then we all lose. Every single last one of us.

3

A Black Latina Woman In Comedy Is No Laughing Matter: Aida Rodriguez

I became acquainted with Aida Rodriguez through Twitter when she read an article I wrote on black celebrities' and social activism in March 2015. After a few email exchanges, I wanted to gain her perspective of how the intersections of her identity affected her professional space in comedy. Rodriguez was kind enough to indulge me, and enlighten us all two months later in May 2015, on the subject of being black, a Latina, and a comedian.

Kovie Biakolo: Aida, can you tell us a little bit about yourself? How did you first get into comedy? What are you most known for? What has been your greatest accomplishment so far?

Aida Rodriguez: I grew up in Miami, Florida. I am of Puerto Rican and Dominican heritage, and my stepfather is Cuban, so I single-handedly represent the entire Spanish-speaking Caribbean. My mother's family first migrated to the Northeast from Puerto Rico during the '50s – my grandmother landed in America in the midst of segregation.

I have always enjoyed making others laugh, I have always wanted to be a comedian since I was a little girl. I used to sneak and listen to Richard Pryor albums and Alvarez Guedes in Spanish. My mother recalls that I when I was little that I would walk around with a broomstick as as my microphone of choice, entertaining her during her harsh pregnancy.

I am most known for my real and no-nonsense approach to life within my brand of humor. Keenan Ivory Wayans once referred to me as being "like a dose of truth serum." I discuss issues of race, motherhood, womanhood and humanness from my most personal place, pointing out the things that many of us think, and are afraid to say.

Though many may believe that my greatest accomplishment is being on a nationally televised show that broadcasts before millions of people, I have to admit that the thing I am most proud of in life is raising two self-aware, evolved, intelligent and compassionate humans. My children are two people that I would want to be friends with if they weren't my children. Together, I dare not undermine their role in this, we have broken many generational cycles that have been destructive and hurtful for family.

KB: What is your experience, firstly, of being a woman in comedy? What are the challenges that you have faced? In terms of your identity as a black, Latina woman in the comedic scene, how have those identities been represented or been received in the space that you work?

AR: Being a woman in comedy is like being a woman in any other male dominated field: You have to work twice as hard, have to be twice as good, to get 70% of the pay. (LOL) But seriously, we aren't afforded the opportunity to be mediocre. Not that I would want to be, but that just isn't there for a woman. Though we are making strides because of women like Roseanne Barr, Sarah Silverman, Amy Schumer, and Wanda Sykes, we still have a ways to go. Being a woman in comedy is a different reality – we are bit more vulnerable on the road in terms of safety and are subject to immediate discrimination. I can't tell you how many people will say to me after a show, "I normally don't like female comedians because they just aren't funny, but you were funny." It's so offensive to hear but I guess you're supposed to take that as a compliment.

Being a woman of color has always been my reality, pointed out early on by my stepfather's Cuban family. I have always operated from the knowledge that people are aware of my color. Colorism exists in a different capacity in the Latino community, and to yet another degree to the white Cubans in Miami. Being told things like my skin color was a stain and that I had scabies because I wasn't white forced me to learn about myself and my history for my own emotional survival. The distinction that Puerto Ricans and Dominicans leaned more towards black – as if it were a negative – was made aware, and that just didn't sit well with my intelligence or humanity.

In terms of the comedy scene, you can feel the segregation at times and you have to make the decision of who you want to be, and I decided some time ago that I was going to be a comedian that happened to be a woman of color, not the other way around. In comedy people tend to challenge everything. It is in the realm of humorous philosophy, and people remain in constant thought.

I have been questioned by some of my Mexican colleagues about my identity while at the same time they have pointed out my blackness. I learned a long time ago that I write my own story, and by knowing my history, I operate from the best place. So nothing can disturb that. I have no problems doing the "black" rooms, "Latino" rooms and mainstream rooms. It is my job!

KB: Can you talk a little bit more about that – blackness in the Latino/a identity? It is something that rarely gets into mainstream conversation. In the first place, the identity of "black Latino/as," and then secondly, the experience. I am specifically referring to notions of anti-blackness within the Latino community, that you have also mentioned. How do you deconstruct it or discuss it in your comedy or what is the specific role, if any, in your politics and your work?

AR: I actually delve into issues of blackness within the Latino community aggressively. I believe that comedy is a safe place to discuss all of the things that make us tick within our society.

I have a joke that takes on the African Diaspora as an attempt to bring forth awareness, and I dared to do it on NBC's *Last Comic Standing*. I believe that race can be our greatest distraction and division, but we cannot ignore that the Latino community is affected by this. There is a big group of Latinos that are not represented in the media. Have you ever seen a black Dominican family TV show? The stigma of being black can be painted so negatively that many immigrants don't want to identify with it, not just Latinos. One of my childhood Haitian friends refused to identify as Black. It was baffling to me a young kid. As I grew up I began to understand that what he perceived to be black was also negative. That exists throughout Latin America – the issues of being a black Latino is not on the agenda of many Latino discussions.

KB: Who would you say are your heroes, both in your life and in the comedic scene? Who are the people that you think really affected and/or continue to affect your style?

AR: No one has influenced my comedy more than my family. Had there been cameras on us growing up, we would be a hit television show. I can tell you that I love the greats in comedy like every other comedian, but the people who really made me laugh were the real ones in my life. Watching my grandmother and mother, both single moms at one time, deal with poverty, racism, and hardship through humor really shaped who I am as a comedian and as a woman. We would find the humor in any and every thing for our survival.

Listening to my stepfather's crazy point of view on life was funnier than any comedy show, but my brother is probably the funniest person in my family without trying to be. The funny has always been around. I chose to focus on it instead of the drama, which was also abundant in my life. Now that we're clear on that, I will say that I love the guys that really pushed it, pushed it far and in your face like Richard Pryor, George Carlin and I continue to be inspired by people like Kathleen Madigan, Louis CK, Bill Burr, Dave Chappelle and Chris Rock. These are the people who grant me permission to play in that space that isn't afraid of "going there," which is code for fucking being real.

Now, I am a lady (Ha!) and I love dressing up, wearing makeup, and being dolled up on stage, so then there is also a list of women that have also granted me a permission of another kind. I can't give you a list of influences without saying Joan Rivers, Rita Rudner, Carol Burnett, Sommore and Lucille Ball.

KB: Can you give examples of what have been the most challenging experiences in your work with regard to your performance as comedian with those identities? Has there been backlash in terms of some of the political statements that you've made or things along those lines?

AR: There is always backlash, even more so now with this internet thing. I have been accused of being harsh, mean, aggressive (as if it's a bad thing) and most of all, racist. I have received death threats and wishes because of my stance on the glorification of celebrity in this country. My jokes have really been a heavy, disturbing thing to some people. I always warn people at my shows that I talk about "everyone" so that no one feels special and give them the option to leave.

There are places and bookers that won't hire me because they don't like my brand of humor. To some of these bookers, "I'm offensive" and not funny. I choose to go where "I'm celebrated, not tolerated" because there are many people that enjoy my style and come see me and they are who I work for. My job is to make people laugh and still be a voice.

I think it's the racism and sexism that resides within these individuals that drives them to discriminate against me and people like me – I know it is. "The audacity of this woman of color to say some of these things is just unbelievable and downright outrageous." They are unaware of their shit. It's not my job to reinforce stereotypes about women and people of color to provide comfort for ignorance. Listen: I stand for something, I am a believer of values and fight for them in an unorthodox manner. If that is offensive to you, go watch someone else.

KB: Can you tell me a little more about your activism and what your goals are, as well as your sociopolitical attitudes that tie in with your work as a comedian and writer?

AR: I am very interested in constantly being involved in the community and working with the youth. (But not interested in drawing media attention to these things.) I was homeless once and it didn't feel very good so the thought of posting, telling, announcing that I am helping other humans makes it feel cheap to me. I don't want to further humiliate someone while they're down – I know the feeling. I do the basic stuff like feeding and clothing the homeless, but I don't really like to talk about that; it's weird, so I won't.

I speak at schools about self-esteem and self-programming, I make sure that when I am performing at colleges that I have a message for those impressionable, hungry minds that are seeking knowledge and awareness.

I believe it is important to go out and speak to young women about image, the media, and the many factors which affect our self-esteem. Specifically young women of color who are not equally represented in mainstream media.

I also suffered from many destructive eating habits which were formed during my stint with the modeling scene, and so I also speak about and incorporate in my comedy the many harmful messages that are constantly being sent to women about weight and appearance.

I believe that my show *Truth Serum* is a form of activism as it is not another comedic show for the sake of comedy, and I wanted it that way. I use it as a platform to discuss those topics and issues that affect us all from a very honest and thoughtful place. I bring in activists, celebrities, personalities to discuss these things as opposed to the typical "I am awesome, my life is great and I have a lot of things" interviews that are so commonplace.

KB: What does the future have in store for you as far as your work in comedy, writing, and as an activist?

AR: I look forward to having a fruitful career in truth, being a voice of the people, and remaining there with them. My writing will continue to be a tool to create opportunities for myself and others – this is not just about me. I will tell the stories through writing jokes, movies, and stories that will bring forth awareness and solutions to mend and bridge. We gotta be here, so why not make it a better place? There will be a space for me and my story on a more visible level, and I look forward to taking that as a duty and responsibility to exalt all of the work and sacrifices made by that little Puerto Rican family that raised me! Agape.

4

Why Does Tess Holliday, The Size 22 Model, Make Us Uncomfortable?

In the late spring of 2015, Tess Holliday caused quite a stir when she was signed to Milk Model Management, becoming the biggest plus-sized model in a mainstream modeling agency. Famous for her size, Holliday was at the center of social conversations of beauty, the modeling industry, health, obesity, fat shaming, the fat acceptance movement, etc. Wanting to get to the root of our societal scrutiny of Holliday and her body, in late May 2015, I engaged Jordan Parker, who is, for the sake of full disclosure, my friend and former group strength training coach. Parker is a health and fitness professional (and environmental activist) in Chicago. Together, we deconstructed some of the social conversations surrounding Holliday and the cultural conversations her visibility raised.

Kovie Biakolo: Hi, Jordan, can you tell us a little about your-self: your background in health, fitness, etc.?

Jordan Parker: Sure. I was an asthmatic child with quite a few health problems – allergies, eczema, etc. – and got into sports when I was really young. It was incredibly helpful for my self-esteem and made me feel "normal" and powerful. I've been active my whole life. I started competing in triathlons in my early 20s and became a personal trainer and fitness instructor shortly after. I worked in the fitness industry for over 15 years.

For several years I taught classes full-time, specializing in high-intensity interval training, strength training, and indoor cycling. I worked with clients one-on-one for many years previous to that, and then found the energy and community of classes more exciting. I've always been a big proponent of strength training for all populations. It's important from a health perspective and also from a psychological one. Being strong physically has always helped me be stronger mentally.

KB: Getting right to it: Tess Holliday has received a lot of media attention. Firstly with her #effyourbeautystandards campaign, and secondly making strides in the modeling world. What is your first reaction to the unceasing talk about her body?

On one hand, it seems like there are people who believe that this is really breaking barriers in terms of body acceptance or body diversity as far as media representations are concerned. On the other hand, there are people who are saying that her being in such spotlight "promotes" obesity. What are your thoughts?

JP: When I first saw photos of Tess Holliday, it was pretty shocking, of course. I can understand why she is getting the attention she is – because she is extreme. We Americans love our extremes. Not only is she overweight, or obese; she is *morbidly* obese. So of course this is going to get some attention. I think it's important to identify what her message is. From the little I've read about her – interviews and pieces – it seems that her message is more along the lines of "Fuck you all, I'm fat and I love it!" rather than "I'm fat and I'm healthy." There is a big difference there.

"Fat shaming" is definitely something we hear a lot about these days, and I can understand the issue. On one hand, every person has a right – and a duty – to accept and love themselves for exactly who they are. This internal acceptance and validation is critical for all of us. I'm not sure if Tess's message is that she truly loves herself – and she is validating herself from within – or if she is looking externally for validation around being morbidly obese.

If she has come to love herself, I say more power to her. It is from this place of self-love that we can actually make the most powerful changes. I have seen many obese and morbidly obese people struggle in the gym and in their lives because they hate themselves for being fat. Paradoxically, if they can accept and love themselves for who they are – fat or not – it makes losing the weight all that much easier. I've seen it.

If people who are obese/morbidly obese can find this place of internal validation and acceptance, then their lifestyle and weight becomes *their* choice; not society's. I think this is one of the big issues here: obese and morbidly obese people feeling the massive amount of pressure and shame from society to be thinner.

In a large sense, Tess is "taking back the control" of her body through her modeling. Whether or not this is really what is going on psychologically for her, I'm not sure. Regardless, the images send the message that she is okay in her body and it's *her* body; she can do what she wants to with it. She gets to decide. And I think that is a good thing.

Another angle in terms of the message her images are sending, however, is that it is just another form of fetishization and commodification of female sexuality. Tess Holliday's images are really no different than anorexically-thin or airbrushed models: it's just the other end of the spectrum. Either end of the spectrum does a disservice to "beauty standards," because regardless of what is happening at the extremes the average woman lies somewhere in the middle – and that is what we don't see very much.

About as many women look like Tess Holliday as look like Gisele, at least in my opinion. The average woman is still not represented and seen as "beautiful." She has to be either a perfected version of herself or an extreme/garish caricature of herself – she can't just be herself. That is too boring and "normal," I suppose, at least in the media. As far as Tess Holliday "promoting obesity"…I don't think people watching her get to decide what she does or doesn't promote. She is presenting an image, and we get to decide how we interpret it.

KB: I really liked what you had to say about the notions of America's extremes. It's something that, as an outsider who is invested in the culture looking in, I am constantly informing people of this perspective. It's not just limited to health, fitness, and wellness. I do have this theory that some people are "angry" at Tess or at the industry or at the situation for this lack of "average-" sized bodies.

But I also wonder if some of this anger or displeasure or discomfort with Tess receiving this media attention comes from something else, maybe a certain societal envy, if you will. People who are eating healthy and are fit and are, in general, conscious of their body in a positive way are *not* necessarily rewarded as perhaps someone who they deem is not "worthy" of this attention. Because they, according to society's rules, are doing the "right things" for their body, and just on face value, Tess supposedly isn't. What do you think about that? Do people just feel that the "wrong person" is being rewarded?

JP: I think as we starting to dig into the layers of meaning and dynamics going on in society at large, this topic becomes fascinating pretty quickly. You're definitely on to something when you talk about society's "anger." I agree, it's much more than just being dissatisfied by truly "average bodies" being underrepresented in the media.

Two things came to me when I read your question. The first is that I think one source of this anger comes from people looking for external validation for their appearance. I'll use myself as an example. For all of my 20s and a large portion of my 30s a *primary* motive of mine to work out was to be attractive and "hot" in society's eyes. My intensity working out – and my motivation to work in the fitness industry – largely came from a place of feeding off that external validation I got for looking great in my size 2 Lululemon.

It wasn't until I tore my ACL in a fluke accident and was forced to take some time off that I really went in-depth into who I am and what my motives really are. From the thousands and thousands of people who I personally trained and taught in my fitness classes, I can say first hand that the majority of them wanted to look good to others, and that was a primary motive for coming to the club or the class.

I also noticed an intensity among women who were in their 30s and 40s and starting to experience some of the natural progression of aging. There was almost an obsession with pre-serving youth, with showing up and working out hard every day in an attempt to compete with the nubile 20-somethings next to them on a bike or a mat. I also worked in high-end clubs like Equinox where you would be likely to find a Gisele next to you in yoga but absolutely not a Tess Holliday.

So what I'm saying is when our motive for working out is pri-marily to look good to the world, there is a sense of weak-ness and judgement that comes along with that. Because we're always looking for external validation, we're constantly sizing up the "competition." Now I work out because it's good for me and I love how it makes me feel more than anything. I'm not attached to the size of my little workout outfits or the feed-back I'm getting on my body. I'm not attached to the "scene" in a particular class or the status of being "FNC" ("Front And Center" – it's true, this is actually a "thing").

I feel more comfortable in my body and less attached to what people think about it. And because of this, I'm much more easy-going and accepting of the Tess Hollidays of the world, because I'm me, and she is her, and that is okay. When we stop looking externally for validation and attention, we become less concerned about who else is getting attention.

The second thing that I thought about when I was reading your question is the work ethic in America. We have an idea that work should be rewarded, and when someone is obese or morbidly obese, we assume that they aren't putting in the work. We assume that they're not physically active, but it also goes beyond that. We also assume that they are just lazy period, and aren't being "productive." I think this is another thing that makes us "angry." We feel that we should be rewarded for being "healthy, productive, and working hard," while obese and morbidly obese people should not.

KB: So many excellent points and ones that definitely crossed my mind as I was thinking about and reflecting on this topic. I do want to ask about these preconceived notions we have about appearance and health. I think people who are ade-quately educated on health and fitness know that "health" does come in different sizes, but the question I have is can health really come at *any* size? I am admittedly skeptical that it can.

Beyond that, too, I have my qualms with the so-called "fat acceptance" movement. Notwithstanding there is something to be said about fat prejudice that I think we all grow up with. Perceiving American culture outside of a citizen's perspective, I do think that I grew up in a home and a culture where to me, this movement seems quite politically correct, and isn't necessarily achieving the outcome – health – that we can all agree is most important in conversations about body.

So, what, if any, are the misconceptions about "being healthy at every size?" Is it really that "fat acceptance" becomes not a way to end fat shaming but rather a way of glorification of fat? (And should "fat" be glorified? Are we prejudiced if we don't think it should?)

JP: This is such an interesting topic – we could talk about this for hours! Health absolutely cannot come "at any size." Can someone be "healthy" and be carrying around a few extra pounds? Absolutely! Can someone be "healthy" and be obese or morbidly obese? Absolutely not. First let's just talk about the logistics of being obese or morbidly obese for a minute. There is the physical limitation of just moving all that flesh around, unfortunately.

Let's be honest: Tess is not going to be riding a bike, jogging or hiking anywhere. Her range of motion and flexibility are severely compromised simply because there is so much fat on her skeleton. Logistically, being that large severely inhibits a person's ability to move, and if you can't move, that's a major health problem. Human beings aren't designed to sit or lie around all the time. Moving keeps us healthy. This is probably the primary reason why obesity and morbid obesity are directly linked to a whole litany of health issues: high blood pressure, heart disease, diabetes, osteoarthritis, stroke, cancer, etc. etc.

When we see someone like Tess Holliday, can we assume that she is most likely completely sedentary and unhealthy? Yes. We can assume that. It's the same as assuming a person in a wheelchair cannot walk. What we cannot assume, however, is that her physical state is entirely within her control or is necessarily her choice.

There are so many reasons why someone may be obese or morbidly obese. For example, childhood obesity is at an all-time high in this country, and it is extremely likely that those children will all become obese and morbidly obese adults. (Plenty of research indicates that a person's metabolism and "set point" are blueprinted in childhood and adolescence. Therefore, if a child is obese or morbidly obese it will take a Herculean effort or surgery to be lean and fit as an adult.)

If a child was less fortunate in the genetic lottery and was raised in an environment where inactivity, sugar, and stress were all staples, can we really assume his or her obesity is a choice? I stop short of saying anyone is a victim – because I fundamentally believe anyone can change – but the cards are definitely stacked against some people, starting in utero. We all have advantages and disadvantages physically and environmentally just like we do socioeconomically.

What I've seen happen is that overweight children or adults

often cross the threshold into obesity or morbid obesity, and when this happens they enter a series of feedback loops that are almost impossible to reverse. Once you have reached a certain body fat percentage, it becomes harder and harder to physically move. Then you become less active and gain more weight and then you become even less active…you see where this is going. Rather than criticize Tess Holliday, we should be criticizing parents who allow their children to sit on their devices all day and eat crap.

What we may see as a "fat acceptance" or "glorification of fat" movement is, in my opinion, really about validation rather than fat. Because fat is so visible, and we live in a corporeal world, people who are obese or morbidly obese face so much more discrimination than someone struggling with a mental health issue who can mask it from society. Or, someone who is anorexic whose clothing covers up the protruding bones.

I think one of the biggest problems here is the assumption we make surrounding an obese or morbidly obese person's *worth* as a person and control over their lives and bodies. Are they most likely sedentary? Sure. You can see that. Are they unhealthy? Absolutely. Is it as simple as them "getting off their asses and going to the gym"? Hell, no. Besides genetics and childhood obesity, mental health is another important variable to consider. We all know someone who could easily be diagnosed with Narcissistic Personality Disorder, but if that person is our boss, our president, or even just an interesting friend, we're so much more forgiving of their neuroses.

If someone self-medicates with food and alcohol and happens

to wear it on their body every day for everyone to see, we feel entitled to come down on those people harder than everyone else. We're blind to many of the issues that are rampant in our society, but because fat is so visible we hone in on that.

KB: I have to wrap this up otherwise we'll be here for ages. And I definitely agree with a lot of what you say. But in comparison with many cultures, I think that American culture really needs a societal reflection on food and its relationship with food because the reality is many countries and cultures don't suffer from this health problem. (Even where there are those who do.) But again, it might be an intercultural prejudice I have, too, especially coming from a home and culture where food is enjoyment but it is not medication or a source of abuse. Ultimately I think "excess" and "extremes" is the norm in much of American food culture.

Now all that aside, and this may seem contradictory after we've just analyzed the implications of Holliday's media attention, but should we even care? Are we "allowed" to care about the size of other people's bodies? It seems to me that you can't have this conversation without ultimately bordering on policing women's bodies which I think society does a "good" enough job of that already.

Is it problematic to have this conversation, and do we ultimately mask our concern for Tess's body as a health concern, when really we're just engaging in a certain kind of policing? For what it's worth, I think the two aren't mutually exclusive, and I think the conversation can be a good one. I also fear that not only the intentions might be impure in some of these public conversations, but the consequences amount to negative outcomes for how we look at and talk about women's bodies which always seem to have such a strict gaze. In those important and famed words, "The body is not an apology."

JP: I completely agree with you that the line between healthy discourse and policing – particularly women's bodies – is often a blurry one. Bring up the topic of breast implants, Botox or any other type of cosmetic surgery and see what happens. I think that every creator of content and viewer of content is entitled to engage in discussion about that content; we are all active participants in the ongoing creation of our cultural narrative.

That being said, I think simply discussing the difference between analysis and policing is a very effective way of identifying the latter. Tess has put herself out there and by nature wants people to talk, and I think this is a positive. Where it becomes negative is when people make assumptions about the internal life of Tess beyond the images we are viewing. We can fairly accurately assume that she is inactive due to the sheer amount of mass she is carrying around, and we can also correctly assume that being morbidly obese is unhealthy.

The emotional reactions around these images, however – "Tess is a fat pig, she has no business getting attention" – are really what we should be examining. As I mentioned, obesity and morbid obesity are complicated issues. It's not just a matter of being lazy or gluttonous. Has anyone considered that perhaps Tess has gone through life not feeling seen, and this is the first shot she's had at really feeling seen? Isn't that what all of us want in some way, to be seen for who we really are and not our external beauty, status in our professions or bank accounts?

We absolutely have a right to discuss Tess's images, but we don't have a right to decide how she became the way she is, what her psychological landscape is like, or her intrinsic worth as a person. Some people may claim that we do have a right to police "unhealthy" behaviors such as smoking, obesity, sedentary lifestyles, etc. "They are all burdens on the health care system" is one argument. I agree, those things are burdens on the healthcare system.

But especially in this addicted, extreme, overworked society, do we have a right to place ultimate value judgements on other peoples' lifestyles as if we know what it's like to be them? Maybe some people just can't handle life without a cigarette. Is that much different from someone buying wine and cupcakes at Whole Foods and indulging in front of the TV to "unwind?" Maybe being morbidly obese feels like a life sentence to Tess, and it's actually the best that she can do. Maybe she's come to terms with who she is and wants to be seen for more than just her body. And that is something I think all of us can relate to.

5

Social Media And Goodbyes: Why Ending Romantic Relationships Is Harder Than Ever

The reality TV show Tough Love *aired on VH1 in March 2009 and would last four years and six seasons. It was the brainchild of expert matchmaker, Steve Ward. Ward's no-nonsense, tell-it like-it-is love coaching style is something many either really love or really hate. Either way, Ward was the perfect person to have a conversation with regarding one of the most difficult parts of any romantic relationship – the ending. In particular, I wanted to find out how social media had changed or had the potential to change the notion of an "ex," in the age of digital culture. In the early summer of 2015, Ward and I engaged in a tough dialogue on love, sex, and relationships.*

Kovie Biakolo: Hello, Steve, could you tell us a little bit about yourself, what you're known for, and what you do for a living?

Steven Ward: Hello, thanks for the opportunity to chat today. I'm a second generation professional matchmaker and the Founder CEO of Love Lab, a free mobile app for creating trust with people before you date.

KB: The first question I have is: what is an ex in the age of Tinder and social media and hook up culture, etc.? Is an ex always someone we've been in an exclusive relationship with? Has the meaning of "ex" changed, and if so, in what ways?

SW: In my opinion, it's too convenient for people to refer to someone as an ex just because they went on a few dates, met the other person's family or friends, or even in cases where two people developed some kind of romantic, emotional connection. In today's day and age, an ex is someone you're no longer sleeping with.

Intimate connections with people are now more ephemeral than ever before thanks to apps like Snapchat, Whatsapp, etc. If you're looking at who's single today and who's going to be single tomorrow, we have to look at who's causing the resurgence in the category of "dating" in the first place. That's Millenials – 18-24-year-olds aren't necessarily looking for the love of their life at this point, and so when they've slept with someone who they've slept with more than once and "dated" or "hung out" with for a semi-regular or even short period of time, it is safe to say they are "seeing" that person. When you're no longer "seeing" someone you're sleeping with, you can safely say they're an ex.

KB: You talked a lot about sex and the end of the sexual relationship being the ultimate end of a relationship, and therefore use of the word "ex" would be adequate. But in the first place, some would argue that you can be out of a romantic relationship with someone and still be in a sexual relationship with them. And then of course, there are those who don't have sex in their relationships at all. What are the rules in those cases or other exceptional cases?

SW: Correct, but in that context you are in an "open" relationship. They wouldn't be considered an ex because, just by a sexual degree of separation, you can contract an STD from that person since they're free to sleep with whomever they want. That binds you. To unbind yourself from that would be to sever a sexual relationship; ergo an "ex."

For people abstaining from sex before marriage due to tradition, religion or a cultural norm in their world, and they agree with one another that they are "in love" and are exclusively following a path together, but then suddenly, for whatever reason, they consciously uncouple before consummating their relationship, sure, they can be considered an "ex."

KB: It seems to me that you're withholding validation of a couple's relationship based on their sexual relationship. I will be forthcoming in saying that not only do I think that's unfair, I also disagree with it. In your perspective, can you be in love without sex? And if you are in love, is that not enough to validate one's relationship? Certainly, as so many people often engage in these days – you can have sex in a relationship and not be in love and have no intention of falling in love with the person. So how does the latter scenario get more validation than the former?

SW: I believe that a connection between a couple matures into a relationship. It is not fair to say all caterpillars are butterflies, but it's fair to say all butterflies were once caterpillars. If you share a sexual connection absent of love whether you want to validate that connection as a relationship or not, you have created a relationship. There is now a bond that cannot be undone. Until a certain bond is made it cannot be constituted as a relationship. It has never been galvanized. When considering the point of view of the next person, or any subsequent individual in that person's life, they will consider it a relationship if it was consummated and only if.

KB: With disagreements discussed, let's move on. What do you think is the single most difficult aspect of moving on in the twenty-first century? With the new ways we're online, it almost seems as if you can't escape people you dated or even people you liked and it failed. How do we move on from people in this day and age? I think many would agree that it just seems harder than ever.

SW: This is an easy question. Our single biggest fear is how we will be perceived by others. When people overexpose themselves and their relationships, they invite judgement and criticism of others. Invariably people will form opinions because you have asked them to. When you air your laundry, express your excitement, share disappointment, etc., you are now asking people to perceive you a certain way. Suddenly, when relationships end, those perceptions are no longer in your control.

Now you must scramble to save face and do your best to enlist the support of friends you shared and people you both know. In short, social media, and technology in general, has greatly impaired our abilities to control what's beyond control. I won't even get started on public shaming or revenge porn.

KB: What is the healthiest way to get over an ex? And do we ever really get over everyone we've dated? Are there some people who are just with us, of whom the possibility of being with them always haunt us, even if we're happy and have moved on?

SW: Enlist a support group and force yourself back out there. In the words of my mom Joann Ward, the original Master Matchmaker, "The best way to get over a woman is to get under a woman." But seriously, if you can't seem to stop thinking about someone or you can't move on, it is more important to understand what is causing the block rather than on how to get past it. Once you realize why you are hung up on that person you can formulate a plan to move on. That process will involve a catharsis of sorts. After that release, it will be possible to compartmentalize the relationship and appreciate it for what it was: a valuable learning experience.

KB: "The best way to get over a woman is to get under a woman." Okay, I have heard this said a number of times and I definitely have to say it deeply worries me. Don't you think that in some ways you use people as medicine for your pains in this way? That doesn't seem fair or right to me. Isn't the better thing to do to spare other people from your pain? You could end up hurting people by "getting under them."

SW: Misery loves company. Distractions are a great way to dissipate stress, tension and anxiety. These feelings usually come in waves that rise and subside. Once they're gone you're able to think more clearly and calmly. Even if you are still in pain, as long as you are straightforward and honest about where you are emotionally, and the fact that you're unavailable, then that person you wish to seek comfort with can choose whether or not they want to proceed at their own risk.

KB: The next question I have is gendered and in the context of heterosexual relationships: do men and women differ in how they perceive "exes" in your opinion? And what are the ways you see they deal with past relationships or past loves differently, if any?

SW: No, I don't believe it's gendered, I believe it's gerontological. Ultimately it depends on how old you are. I think younger people, Millennials, consider an ex to be someone they were sleeping with for a period of time. I think the older you get the more substantive it would have to be. As people mature they raise the bar in terms of what they'd qualify as a relationship. Relationships are measured by one's own prior experience. A one year relationship seems like an eternity to someone who's never had a relationship last more than 6 months. But to someone who has had relationships last more than a couple of years, a one year relationship doesn't seem long at all.

KB: In terms of so-called hookup culture that Millennials tend to "suffer" from, if you will, how do you think that affects our ability to move on from relationships and into new relationships? Is it a hindrance? Does it help? Does everything depend on context?

SW: Romantic connections are becoming more and more ephemeral. It's making relationships feel more disposable than ever. I think it's going to affect young people's ability to weather storms in their relationships. If anything, it gives people the ability to learn and discover what they do and don't like. The more experience one has, the greater their ability to make sound decisions and exercise good judgement in the future. Without bad experiences you can't fully appreciate the good ones. This ephemerality is reducing the equity people place in their relationships. This diminishes the potential for success from the start. Without at least the perception or intent to make connections evolve long-term, they rarely stand a chance to.

KB: What do you think is the most important thing everyone should know about moving on from people? If you could make one grand, big statement about it, what would you say? What advice would you give to anyone going through that right now?

SW: I'd say that if you feel despondent, alone, isolated, and scared, take solace in the fact that billions and billions of people have experienced those very same feelings before. Find support from those people and focus on positive, uplifting activities. Re-apply your newfound availability to invest in passion projects, interests or endeavors you put off for too long. Look at this time in your life as a period of rediscovery and a chance to start fresh and anew.

KB: Finally, a cliche'd question but ultimately one that does have to do with exes: Is it *really* better to have love and lost than never to have loved at all, in your opinion?

SW: Absolutely. A clichéd question deserves as clichéd response. If I fall out of love 999 times in my life but fell in love 1,000 times I will have died a happy man.

6

Everything You Think You Know About The Homeless Is Wrong

Homelessness occupies a complex reality and perception in the United States. Depending on where one lives, it can be both heavily stigmatized while also highly visible. Kavita Das, a New York-based writer who has been featured in The Atlantic and NBC Asian America, among many other places, also has a professional background in working for social change. Das and I broke down the myths, facts, and grey areas of homelessness in America in July 2015.

———

Kovie Biakolo: Hello, Kavita, can you tell us a little about yourself and your background in urban planning and working with the homeless?

Kavita Das: Hi, Kovie. I worked in the social change sector for about 15 years and I started out my career working on special needs housing for the City of Philadelphia. I've never struggled with homelessness personally, and I mention that because I think the perspective of people who have struggled with or are currently struggling with homelessness is an important one. In my role, I helped support transitional housing programs for people with various special needs including those who had disabilities or had HIV/AIDS.

KB: We hear so many different statistics and narratives about homelessness regarding causes and consequences and how many stay homeless, its relationship with mental illness, etc. Now I have never worked with the homeless in any professional capacity. My experiences have been limited to volunteering, my everyday interactions, and what I know from a few studies I have read and analyzed. My first question is: what are the biggest misconceptions about homelessness that we come across every day?

KD: One common misconception is that there are only homeless individuals not homeless families. And similarly, people think that it's not possible for a middle-class family to become homeless. However, families can become homeless and end up in the shelter system because of a lost job or a health care crisis. Another frustrating misconception is that homeless individuals want to be homeless or that they are too lazy to find employment. One of the biggest drivers to chronic homelessness is untreated mental health or substance abuse issues.

KB: I'm glad you mentioned mental health because that is the capacity in which I have most been familiar with homelessness. However, with both homeless people I have interacted with and recently when I saw a post on Humans of New

York, one of the stereotypes that people who are homeless face is that others think they are *always* suffering from mental illness. (Or substance abuse, as you said. But the stereotype that seems to get the most complaints is the former.) So, what do you know as fiction and what is fact, when it comes to how mental illness and homelessness are related?

KD: Well, as I understand it, the link between mental health issues and homelessness is a strong but complex one. First, there is a distinction between those individuals who are chronically homeless and those who are temporarily homeless. Some individuals who are chronically homeless are dealing with serious mental health issues and may have been in and out of the mental health system and even the criminal justice system. They face the double stigma of having a mental health issue and being homeless. But it's also important to note that anyone and probably everyone can and will face mental health crises, and if you have a strong support network, you tend to have better outcomes.

KB: Stepping away from mental illness and homeless, can you speak to the relationship between LGBTQ youth and homelessness? I have heard and read limited information about the relationship, but it does seem like a particular concern. What is known (and unknown) about how and why many LGBTQ youth are said to make up a large portion of the homeless communities across the United States?

KD: Yes, LGBTQ youth are a part of the homeless population, particularly in big cities. They are often underage and don't have support networks because they've either been kicked out of their homes or run away from home because they don't feel accepted by their families because of their gender/sexual identity, and they can be vulnerable to sexual abuse and prostitution. I'm happy to see that there is greater awareness and support for at-risk and homeless LGBTQ youth through initiatives like Ali Forney Center, Cyndi Lauper's True Colors Fund, Miley Cyrus's Happy Hippie Foundation, and organizations like F.I.E.R.C.E. that specifically do outreach to LGBTQ youth of color.

KB: Can you speak to some of the differences in homeless in the United States as opposed to in other places in the world? Some places, for example, have what is called a "begging culture" while other places seemingly have a true, authentic "homeless community" in their cities. How do different places in the United States compare to other parts of the world? Also, the United States is often seen as doing relatively poorly in comparison to other countries in the West. Is that solely a function of the way our social systems work with regard to employment and indeed to mental health?

KD: Well, broadly I do believe that the level of homelessness in a society or in a city is a barometer for how well or poorly it is doing in terms of providing accessible mental health services, job opportunities, job training, prison re-entry support, affordable housing…essentially it's a barometer of how well the safety net works for the most vulnerable. And although homelessness has decreased nationally, it is still high in many cities. Here in NYC, it has tripled from 1985 to today. According to the Coalition for the Homeless, there are close to 60,000 people sleeping in NYC shelters each night. And this doesn't include those who are sleeping on the streets of the city. So New York City has not been able to effectively address homelessness in part because it hasn't addressed the issues above.

In terms of the United States versus other parts of the world, there are definitely some cities around the world where begging is more prevalent. I spent many childhood summers in Calcutta and begging by adults and children was heartbreakingly prevalent, but then again, I remember living in Paris as a college student and seeing French individuals begging on the Metro. But as a lifelong New Yorker, the rise in homelessness is very troubling both in terms of the statistics as well as what is evident when you walk around the streets of the city.

KB: One of the questions that people always ask – well, well-meaning, decent people is, "How can I help the homeless person in front of me?" I'm going to leave out the people who say things such as, "If homeless people wanted a job, they'd have one." I'm talking about people who are somewhat aware of homelessness but who know the relationship between homelessness and substance abuse especially – how can people help the person in front of them, either monetarily or otherwise?

KD: All I'll say about the latter, uncharitable group of people is that many people were against food stamps until they themselves needed them during the recent recession. In terms of how to help the homeless, it's certainly something that I think about and there's no simple or one-size-fits-all answer. I have one friend who started an organization to throw birthday parties for children in homeless shelters and I know writers and artists who do art therapy for homeless children. But when confronted by a homeless individual, I think it's important to look at them and to see them and not briskly walk by because of what it communicates to them and to ourselves about their importance in this world. Personally, I don't typically give money but if I feel comfortable, I ask them if they would like a cup of coffee or some food.

KB: Lastly, what would you like people to always remember about homelessness? One of the things that is a reality for many Americans, especially given the political and social systems, is that many people are "one paycheck," "one medical disaster," and "one failed support system" away from homelessness. Knowing this, I have always found it necessary to show compassion to the homeless. But I sometimes feel that this fear is what actually drives people to have such hardened attitudes towards the homeless. So, what is the parting advice for us all when we discuss homelessness and/or encounter homeless people?

KD: On a broad level, I think it's important to educate ourselves about the issue by turning to national organizations like National Alliance to End Homelessness as well as to those who are working to fight homelessness on a local level, whether it's a homeless shelter, soup kitchen, or an advocacy organization. But on a more personal level, I hope we can see ourselves in those who are homeless and vice versa, rather than assume that they are somehow different or less than us. I hope we can pause from our hectic lives and look away from our screens and silence our headphones long enough to acknowledge and address their suffering.

7

An Ex-Baltimore Police Officer Discusses Police Brutality And Reform

In April 2015, a series of protests took place in Baltimore after the arrest of Freddie Gray. Gray died one day later from injuries to his spine and neck which were sustained while in the police vehicle upon his arrest. Gray was added to the growing number of high-profile black people who has died from America's increasingly widely-known police brutality problem.

Michael A. Wood, Jr, a retired Baltimore police officer, had long been publicly expressing concern for policing in America. In April 2015, people began listening to Wood on social media. In August 2015, I conversed with Wood to learn more about his perspective on the state of policing in the country.

Kovie Biakolo: Hi, Michael, thank you so much for joining us today. I understand that you are an ex-Baltimore police officer who currently advocates for change in policing and police culture. Could you give us an understanding of your background, what exactly your advocacy is doing, what you want to achieve?

Michael A. Wood, Jr.: Thanks for having me, Kovie. It is this very discussion that my immediate goals are trying to achieve. While it was years and years ago that I started advocating for police reform, I think I was largely blind to the reform being a byproduct of a societal reform that must take place. The second civil rights movement, so to say.

I am the prototype all-American kid by most definitions. I came from a poor family in a mixed neighborhood and fought my way up to the USMC at 17 where I was an Assaultman (bombs & rockets) in the Fleet Antiterrorism Security Team. I then joined the Baltimore Police Department in 2003 because I was always going to be a cop, and let's deal with my honesty – it was fun and thrilling and powerful.

I went to tons and tons of schools, fighting and paying for everything myself, but after completing a Masters and the skills that come along with that, compounded by horrors we see on TV, I really began to critically evaluate what we are fundamentally doing in policing and what result that has. It is clear that result oppresses the most disenfranchised of our people, and we just cannot do it that way. So let's talk, let's improve, and hopefully, people will force the politicians to get me or someone like me in a position to enact reform.

KB: So first thing's first, I wanted to revisit this year's Baltimore uprising or *riot* – the semantics obviously dependent on who you are and your politics. In your opinion, what were the short-term and long-term causes of this? Indeed, Freddie Gray's death was the spark that lit the fire in many people's eyes. But such a reaction does not exist in a vacuum. What caused this, and what do you think was the result? What will history say about it, in 20, 50 years?

__MW:__ I go with uprising, for the record – that's what we are doing right now and that was just a part of that overall societal awakening. The short-term cause of the Baltimore uprising was complete mismanagement by the Mayor, BPD, and Maryland State government. The spark was in Mondawmin mall. In Baltimore, the kids ride public buses, and there is a connecting hub at Mondawmin. Due to poor intell and management, the buses were shut down and kids were trapped there, far from home. Those kids were met by the police surrounding them as an occupying force, trapping them from home, armed, and ready for conflict.

I can't say I would not fight when someone clearly came to fight, especially as a scared kid. Long-term, we are simply boiling over with injustice in America. And really I'm surprised it has taken this long, once I started taking a deeper look. The oppression of the weakest in our society always results in eventual uprising. What is the result, so far? I don't know. Nothing? No one cared about Gilmor homes a week before Freddie Gray and no one cares about it now. It will remain a struggle to fight against this, but I really hope that in 20-50 years, this is seen as the spark to the second civil rights movement.

__KB:__ One of the things you're quite familiar with is the drug trade and how that affects police work and police culture overall. Now, coming from a very social theory perspective, "the war on drugs," and "just say no," seemed to essentially give a reason to police the poor and the disenfranchised even more. Moreover, it seemed to burden those who have the least capabilities into "being responsible" for the negative consequences of drug consumption – which is more of a societal problem, rather than strictly an individual one. Could you please address that – drugs and narcotics – and the relationship between those things and how the police interact with the poor?

MW: Yes, I'm very familiar with the drug trade. I took no less than twenty training courses on narcotics, was a street narcotics enforcement detective then later, and major case narcotics detective before being promoted. What I want to address right away is that there is no reason to sugarcoat it, it does not just *seem* to give the police carte blanche on the disenfranchised – it absolutely does. This is incredibly easy to see in the statistics and just through observation.

Until the war on drugs, the prison population just about mirrored the general population and was then obviously largely white. Since the war on drugs and overcriminalization in general, the institutionalized racism, fear of blacks, and society's overall sentiments about the poor and minorities were given the tools to come to the surface. And we now see the prisons filled with blacks and other minorities.

This is not some strange coincidence. We know that whites, and really any group of humans, use drugs at about the same rate, and always have. Somehow there is now a sickening number of non-violent drug offenders, who are mainly minorities, filling the prisons of the country that imprison more of their citizens, in the land of the free, than any other country.

KB: What, if anything, do you think the public at large would be surprised about with regard to how the police interact with the poor? But aside from that, are there some who believe – with good rationale and argument – that given the history of the police in the country, their essential function are to be the protectors of white supremacy? Do you think that's a valid argument to make, and why or why not?

MW: The public being so surprised is what surprises me most. That surprise is that I am saying that the black community has not been lying to you all of these years. Maybe I thought they were, as well. But over time and seeing it first hand, these stories are true. I do not know of a single report I have made which has not already been stated by someone in a poor community.

Everything you've heard rapped about, written, and spoken that alleges police did some outrageous shit happened somewhere in this country – some of those offenses, an uncountable amount of times. The amount of illegal searches on the black community is staggering. Neil deGrasse Tyson even talks about how often he was approached, and really can we find a better human being on the planet? The crazy part is that for most of white America this concept is foreign, it is even incomprehensible, as the number of illegal searches cannot be calculated in relation to themselves because you cannot divide by zero.

I am not sure that there is a sound argument to the protection of white supremacy as intentional. What I really think is that everything is that way. Everything is structured by the whites who stole this land, imported slaves, and limited rights of minorities, into the very fabric of our functioning of a society. I don't think many individuals are consciously aware of that now, but they are largely carrying out what they have been taught. We are largely taught *what* to think, not *how* to think. Once you critically evaluate how we function in this country, the racism invades everything.

KB: Okay – with regard to the argument of how the history of the police affects the culture today, one of the duties of police during slavery was to catch slaves, so I think it isn't lost in the American imagination that black bodies represent something that is traditionally criminalized. That is to say, the history extends far beyond the war on drugs.

Now given that context, and given that we can barely go a news cycle without some sinister incident where the police and a black body is pronounced dead or something of the sort, are black and brown and poor communities – and how those communities intersect – justified in saying that the police are more bad than good? Are they justified in believing that "good cops" are few and far between, and oftentimes if there are any, they probably leave the job?

MW: I think it is completely a part of the fabric of American society to fear the black person, especially the black man. Where I waver a little is that people fear everything they do not understand. That leads me to question the motivations; maybe the ignorance is the underlying problem. By ignorance, this also carries over into the policy, laws, training, et cetera of law enforcement.

Even in academia, criminal justice is embarrassingly led by ideology and not facts or reproducible science. That ideology at the root of the creation of the criminal justice system is the ideology of ignorant people who feared what they did not understand, what they saw as others, as an inferior species. We know that this is not true – race is just a set of genetic variables. We know that the foundation of criminal justice thinking is flawed, but nothing is being done about it.

To address the second half of that question, I do not have definitive evidence, but I am confident in saying that if I were black and in a poor community, I would be more afraid of the cops than probably anyone else. The lack of accountability may be the largest determiner there, though. The "good" cops are an anomaly.

I was embarrassed and ashamed of myself once I finally started to realize that. The "good" cops, like Joe Crystal, who report things and see them right away, do not last very long – they either quit or get railroaded. There were twelve bad cops in McKinney, not one. ["McKinney" refers to a Texas incident where a white cop sat on a young black girl.] And while my record is impeccable, my resume ideal, I was not a "good" cop when I was in. I had to stand outside of the blue wall before

I saw its immensity, much like how many other members of LEAP explain it as well.

KB: Let's talk a little bit more about LEAP because I think people have a general understanding of what it is – if they know it. But for those who aren't familiar with it, tell us a little bit more. When did it start, what are its aims, etc.?

MW: LEAP is Law Enforcement Against Prohibition and they are comprised of former cops, prosecutors, judges, professors, and more who see the evil of drug prohibition. I have to give the company line, so to say, because I don't have enough experience within the organization to speak authoritatively. They came to me after hearing me speak out so they are obviously paying attention to what is going on. The company line is at leap.cc, but from my experience with the leaders, LEAP was primarily focused on ending the drug war and ending the criminalization of consensual adult agreements, in general.

With the need for complete police reform surfacing, LEAP is looking to expand and I hope to be a large part of that. They were looking for a youth infusion to help guide real reform, and I am trying to fulfill that role. Confidential police reporting of corruption, outside use of force investigations, policy reform, training reform, public speaking, and more are expanding concepts for LEAP. The outside investigations are something that I think is critical and that really needs to be pushed.

KB: That's very good to know. Now, in your opinion, what should ordinary citizens be doing? Sometimes it honestly comes across as there are multiple Americas, and there are a whole lot of people – notably white and oftentimes middle-class – who completely come off as willfully ignorant to the plight of poor communities of color.

It seems almost daunting and discouraging to believe that people aren't aware of what's going on. Or rather, what has always been going but is now more heightened because of social media – which has broken down some of the gate-keeping of traditional media. So why should ordinary, white, middle-class Americans care about this? It's sad I have to ask the question but it seems like it's a question worth asking.

MW: It is a perfect question as it is also where I struggle the most. We have a run of great science communicators which have helped society understand the importance of science. The previously mentioned, Neil deGrasse Tyson, is probably the greatest since Carl Sagan. We need to find a way to be effective communicators of racism and police reform. How do we do that? I am trying desperately to do that. The fine line is what I fear.

When I go with my heart and get ultra-liberal, I'm going to lose those who may have listened because of my physical appearance and service. Conversely, I also need the black community to trust me, to push for me or someone like me to get the power in politics for actual reform. One misspeak and understandably, I could lose that delicate trust.

The ordinary citizen needs to keep this discussion going. I am not saying I am some authority, but listen to what we are saying in the movement. Just give us a minute and I think it becomes very clear for anyone other than those who are just holding onto the bigotry, and sometimes that behavior needs to be treated with ridicule to end. This ignorance you speak of should be ridiculed. And in my opinion, it is completely unacceptable, as the only way to not have empathy for the black community is to be willfully ignorant. I cannot tell you how many family and friends I have lost because of this, but those people are not family or friends.

We should all care about this movement because it is a movement about equality. It is a movement about strengthening the fabric of our society. It is about making less poor people, less problems. It is about becoming one, and using empathy and science to make changes which will improve the safety of everyone in America.

Does white America want to go to Baltimore, watch the fireworks, and not be scared of what can happen? Okay, then let's talk about how to do that and do what actually works, even if that means giving up a little bit of white power and white privilege. Even for a racist white who has that fear of some random black man raping their daughter, that won't happen if he is in college and signing your paycheck.

KB: I guess that's the reality of being in social justice – you'll lose some friends along the way. But I've also always believed that any cause that doesn't cost you something is probably not worth fight for.

Lastly, Michael, what is your vision for the kind of police

reform you seek? And perhaps even more than that, how will this vision affect the kind of America you want to live in? Is there really hope, or are we just caught in a cycle of power where we trade one power holder for another? Can the brutal police culture of this country be transformed, and what will it take?

MW: Being in social justice is something I never thought I would be doing. I was really enjoying my quiet life of school, work, and family. But in this household we all agree that it is worth fighting for. So my vision of perfect policing is decentralized, monitored by the public (yes, I mean with complete access), and problem oriented. That's largely tentative, but we need to study the issue without being clouded by ideology. I really think that this can be accomplished, and it would be really easy if the federal government would make a few painful changes.

The absolute most important issue is ending drug prohibition and over criminalization. Most of the names that we call out, Freddie Gray, Tyrone West, Eric Garner, Sandra Bland, and more can be immediately prevented by taking away some of the policies which enable police to express their own biases and prejudices and then cover them in a veil of legality. The vast majority of police violence and participation in the school to prison pipeline is rooted in drug prohibition.

I have estimated that 90% of my police work was drug-related. The vast majority of "black on black" crime is rooted in the drug trade, just like how so much violence was white on white, during alcohol prohibition. So what about black on black crime? End the drug war. If you care about black on black crime, poverty, oppression, abuse, fatherless homes, et cetera, end the damn war we have on our citizens. That won't end institutionalized racism, but it will take away the biggest facilitator of it.

In order to change the drug policy, we need the people to speak, and the only way I can see that occurring is through a constitutional amendment to take the money out of politics. This is being done at WolfPac and they desperately need your support. The politicians do not serve your interests. I do not care what they tell you, they serve the interest of donors and do you really think the donors care about the oppression of minorities? Step 1: Return the power of the people via Wolf-Pac. Step 2: End drug prohibition. Step 3: Policy reform.

The reason I am pessimistic about change without those things is because it will depend upon the individual politicians making changes. That may work sporadically, but it has no longevity. We need a constitutional amendment to lock in the changes this generation will achieve.

8

Sex, Love, And Tinder Culture: Are Millennials Setting Themselves Up For Failure?

In the spring of 2015, I visited an old college friend who introduced me to the TV show, Married At First Sight. *She thought I might want to write an article on it. Indeed, I found the show interesting – couples quite literally meet on their wedding day. It was the modern, American reality television version of arranged marriages but one that claimed to have the backing of science.*

Sexologist and sex educator Dr. Logan Levkoff is the sexual expert on the show. At a time when Millennials are constantly scrutinized for "hook-up" culture, she is one of the best in the business to discuss the subject. In what became the most popular dialogue of 2015, Dr. Levkoff and I dialogue about Millennials' delicate dating culture.

Kovie Biakolo: Hello, Dr. Levkoff. Can you tell us a little bit about yourself and your background in order to get a better idea of your expertise and knowledge-base?

Logan Levkoff: Hi, Kovie; of course. I am a sexologist and sexuality educator. I started in this field as a peer HIV/AIDS educator when I was 15 years old. I was always comfortable talking about sexuality. I went to college and realized that there were not many public female voices on sex/uality that were positive, candid, and representative of what my peers and I were experiencing.

I tried to fill that void by continuing peer education, writing anonymous sex advice columns, and fairly provocative articles in our campus' women's paper. This was long before campus sex columns were popular. I wound up getting a Masters and Ph.D. in human sexuality education.

I would say that I deal with all aspects of sex and sexuality, but primarily I work teaching kids, teens, and parents – all in an effort to de-stigmatize sex and sexuality and encourage healthy communication about sex. Most recently, I am the sexuality expert on *Married at First Sight*.

KB: That is quite the career path. I would say not a lot of people know what a sexologist is or what they do on a long-term basis. Thank you for informing us. Now to get right to it, let's talk firstly about Tinder culture which has been in the news in interesting ways in the last few weeks.

I will candidly say that I find the general idea of Tinder at best, harmless, and at worst, disheartening. On the one hand,

I understand that we are in a technological generation, on the other, I think it is reducing meeting and mating to ordering a sandwich.

Perhaps there is nothing wrong with it in and of itself, but the way it has been applied seems to be riddled with, for lack of a better word, "interesting" consequences. One of them being people use the app for basically as much sex as possible – even though some may get on it with the intent to date and maybe even to do so on a long-term basis. In the first place, what do you think of when I say, "Tinder culture," and what are your thoughts on it?

LL: Such a good (and complicated) question. Tinder culture: short-term fun but perhaps not satisfying for the long-term. I have no problem with consenting adults having sex or looking for sex without seeking a "relationship."

That being said, I am someone who believes that it is always important to be upfront and honest about what you want. I worry that we have lost some of our ability to speak up for what we want, whether that is no-strings attached sex or a more emotionally intimate relationship. Sexually healthy people acknowledge their needs and aren't afraid to ask for things.

Now, I do think that Tinder is fascinating. I love that dating apps give us the opportunity to meet people we may have never encountered before; however, I would be lying if my heart didn't break a little at the thought of a swipe based on a split second look at someone. Is sexual chemistry and attraction important? Yes. Is is enough to sustain a long-term relationship if nothing else is there? No.

One last thing: did Tinder create the hook-up culture? Certainly NOT. I wrote something on Twitter recently that spoke to this. I wrote: Tinder creating the hook-up culture is like Zima creating teen alcohol use in the 90s. These things already existed. Nothing new.

KB: Let's talk about hook-up culture. And I completely agree, I don't think Tinder created hook-up culture, but it is facilitating it. However, Tinder wouldn't exist without hook-up culture. Hook-up culture is an interesting phenomenon to me.

In order to be forthcoming, I will say I do not participate in it for several reasons. But looking on as an outsider, and an outsider who enjoys analyzing cultural phenomena, I have found that many people who do participate in it do not think of themselves as participating in it. It's almost as if hook-up culture is something that many who participate in it still also want to distance themselves from.

But in light of books like *Sex at Dawn*, it does make it seem like modern-day views on sex prior to hook-up culture were not quite in line with what our ancestors did tens, if not hundreds of thousands of years ago. *Sex at Dawn* contends that contrary to the "common narrative of human sexuality," multiple sexual partners was common and accepted prior to the agricultural revolution in terms of human evolution. The text does this by comparing human mating systems to that of bonobos.

From a research perspective, I dispute some of the claims because the methodology seems to be unjustifiably selective in its sample use of bonobos, and the conclusions are based on a lot of circumstantial evidence. Not only that, but some of it cannot be confirmed by anthropological data and negates the presence of biology and differences that exist in biology.

And I say this as someone who studies culture – but who also knows that sometimes social scientists get in their own way by holding out mere hypotheses as facts. And thus, the notions becomes tantamount to nothing more than pop psychology.

So tell me about hook-up culture, its implications for society, and the consequences of engaging with material such as *Sex at Dawn* without reading or understanding critiques of it.

LL: I have trouble with the whole hook-up culture, mostly because I think that it was a term used to describe what many people do when they are trying to navigate their own sexuality and their desires and feel empowered to do so.

The "HOOK-UP CULTURE" may seem formal now simply because technology has made it more organized, but I struggle with it as a general term or description. I sometimes feel like when people use that term it is done to minimize people's experiences rather than consider that those experiences (satisfying or not) help to create better ideas of what we need and what we want out of our partnerships.

Now, having said that, I have been in a monogamous relationship for 20 years. Do I believe that monogamy is the default "natural state" for all human beings? No.

I think that many people are monogamous because that is what our culture has dictated (regardless of whether or not we agree) and it helps to organize our lives. Of course, this isn't true for everyone. There are many communities where families are blended, shared responsibilities among all people, and polyamory is accepted and respected.

I am a firm believer that anything that initiates a dialogue (ideally an intelligent one) about a subject is valuable. *Sex at Dawn* is one of those texts. It is fascinating and provides us with an opportunity to talk to the people in our lives about expectations in a relationship. I like to think that where I do my best work is helping people to make sense of what is in our culture – pop or otherwise.

KB: I definitely think that the word "natural" being applied to relationships – monogamous and otherwise – is skewed in favor of those who dispute monogamy as natural. This is to say, I think monogamy is natural to human nature, but it is not the *only* natural way to organize human relationships in society.

I know this because I'm an African and on both sides of my family directly, polygamy has been practiced at one point among my recent ancestors, so what I'm trying to say is I don't think it's an either/or thing. I think there is variance in natural occurring phenomenons; I think it is quite possible that there are multiple "natural" existences when it comes to mating in general and especially long-term mating and relationship decisions.

Of course culture dictates and shapes, as well, and I do think that human beings have to be humble to the notion that many of us do not know quite know when the natural starts and stops, and when the cultural starts and stops. I think it is a more prudent position to claim they are intertwined, that there are thin lines, and it probably changes as culture changes, and what we know about the science of the human experience changes.

But I want to get beyond that and get into why I think some of our dating practices may not be in line with long-term social desires. I've been thinking about this idea of the long-term self and the short-term self in many contexts.

Now the idea in this context is that the short-term self wants to engage in as much as "free love" or sex, as possible. But because of culture, many also want committed relationships in the long-term. The idea is, however, that if one pays attention only to the short-term self, is it possible that it comes as a consequence to the long-term self? Does any of that make sense at all?

LL: First, I agree with you on the monogamy issue. Just wanted to get that out of the way. There has never been one way to experience life.

Now, with respect to other issue, I think that I understand what you are getting at. I guess I am wondering: are you referring to emotional intimacy? Childbearing? Partnership in general?

I think that it is very easy for us to get swept up in our current place – whether that is age, expectations of peer group, and so on. While I don't believe that paying too much attention to where we are now irreparably impacts our ability to be satisfied in the future, there is a small caveat to that. Childbearing.

While there are amazing reproductive technologies available to us, they are not simple solutions. I get the feeling that many people are afraid to talk about what they want in the future for fear that they will scare off potential mates, but if I have learned anything over the years, it is that we all have deal breakers.

We need to think about (and be candid about) what those non-negotiables are for us. (Though I would ask people to think about what's behind that deal breaker to determine if it is a preference or if it is at all malleable. If not, that's fine, too.)

KB: Let's move on to our modern conceptions of dating, love, and commitments, including marriage. One of the ways in which culture really affects my perspective is in choosing long-term mates.

Now I have not yet read Aziz Ansari's book *Modern Romance,* although I read his excellent essay about it in *Time,* and I identified with some of what he had to say. When I observe American culture as an African in this context, it seems very romantic to me but not necessarily in a good way.

For all intents and purposes, I am a romantic, but my romanticism does not come at a cost of making practical decisions. For me, commitments ought to involve pragmatism. This notion of fairy tale romance as the sole prerequisite for long-term commitments, especially marriage, is something I look at with a little hesitancy.
Marriages should have at their core, love, but the type of love evolves over time.

I don't think that fairy tale love – which I do not mean to mock but I use in the sense of what our media texts have exposed to – is a guarantor of a lasting-commitment. I think one has to consider everything from (non-) religious values, to children, to the history of someone's family, to career goals, to financial stability, amongst other things.

It sounds entirely unromantic but being the product of a 34+ year marriage if there's anything my parents have insisted on, it's that *just love* isn't going to get you through. Respect and agreements on certain values, but also the little details of pragmatism that I've mentioned are what at least they have seen, makes marriage – which they can speak to – something long-lasting.

What do you think?

LL: Well, I'm not sure I could have said it better myself. I am not a romantic. The fairy tales have never turned me on. Roses and chocolate and jewelry don't turn me on. Respect turns me on. And for me, I believe that respect leads to romance.

When partners feel valued, when their contributions to the relationship – whether those are financial, emotional, household, or familial – are respected, romance blossoms. Marriages should have at their core, love, but the type of love evolves over time. That evolution isn't bad, it's wonderful. It's deep and solid.

Good marriages (or partnerships in general) are grounded in balance and equality, respect, communication, and an understanding of who someone is from a holistic perspective (who they are, where they come from, what they want, what their values are, and so on).

Is passion important? Yes, but the passion that comes from the novelty of a (new) relationship is going to change. If we believe all the headlines on the covers of women's magazines that tell us how to keep things as hot as they were in the beginning, we are in trouble. If things aren't as hot, we may assume that our partnership is failing. You can't assume that. Relationships evolve.

KB: Yes, that absolutely make sense. For the record – I do love flowers though! (Haha) But to wrap this up, one of the things I think about in any cultural conversation that has to do with human beings making personal choices, especially in the context of something as vast and wide as sex and dating and love, is that none of us are unicorns.

I say this because people have this notion that we can simply ignore media texts and history and what we're taught about sex, dating, and love from childhood – regardless of whatever culturally-specific messages we receive. But *we know* that is not possible in its entirety. Those things, even when we go against them are how we fundamentally formed our understanding of the world. Some of them, we might individually and as a society agree are worth changing – or one might disagree.

Are we using our experiences to think about the bigger issues or do we just go through the motions without thinking about what it is we really want or need?

In studying human history and in observing humans, I think there is this generational observation that has been said many times – the solution of one generation becomes the problem of the next. For this culture, the sexual revolution, as it's called, can be said to have fostered some of what we now call hook-up culture – even though as you said, and I think you're right, that term might be limiting.

It seems to me that because none of us are unicorns but culture is also dynamic, we're in this place where on one hand, the previous generation's solution became our "problem" – in the context of hook-up culture, and on the other, we still want to form long-lasting relationships. But I get the sense this is becoming increasingly more difficult with that hook-up cultural norm also being a facet of our generation.

What are we Millennials doing, and what are the consequences of what we're doing?

LL: In general, I would say that participating in anything that doesn't represent you or goes against your personal or cultural values is rarely going to be satisfying. What I would rather do is encourage – and in some cases give Millennials the freedom – to think about what it is that they really want and to not feel guilty if those *wants* are more traditional or more nontraditional.

What many of us do is find ourselves going through the motions because it is easy, and it is what is expected of us. I don't think that there is an official outcome or consequence to participating in a "culture;" experiences give us perspective and ideally help us to determine what it is that we really want out of life, love, and sex.

The question we really need to be asking is: are we using our experiences to think about the bigger issues or do we just go through the motions without thinking about what it is we really want or need?

9

The Never-Ending Problem Of U.S. Mass Shootings And Gun Laws

On October 1, 2015, a mass shooting took place in Umpqua Community College near Roseburg, Oregon. Mass shootings in contemporary American culture appear to occupy a perspective of being both shocking yet commonplace. To engage in discussion, I invited veteran and retired Baltimore Police Sgt. Michael A. Wood Jr. again in Mid-October to dialogue on the contentious issue.

———————

Kovie Biakolo: Hi, Michael. Can you tell us a little about your background and then also tell us what was your primary reaction to the latest major school shooting in Oregon?

Michael A. Wood Jr.: In short, I am a typical rural American. I now have a wife and young daughter and am working on my PhD in Management after serving 4 years in the USMC, 11 years in the Baltimore Police Department, a BS in Criminal Justice, and an MS in IT Management.

My time in Baltimore was ground zero for the gun violence in America. As for the Oregon tragedy, my reaction is sadness, maybe some hopelessness because this is expected, foreseeable, and televised across the world. Meanwhile, mass shootings occur on the regular in poor black communities and no one seems to care.

KB: Before we get to the heart of the conversation which is about gun-related deaths and especially mass shootings, I want to address that latter point. In discussing mass shootings, there is this point that is brought up about shootings that take place in poor, and oftentimes poor, black neighborhoods. These shootings are related to gang activity which is related to economic and social disenfranchisement.

I really think it's important to make that distinction because there are historical and sociological factors that are understood as far as the causes for "shootings in the ghetto" or shootings in poor neighborhoods. These causes are often related to institutionalized racism and a certain lack of upward economic movement for the poor.

Do you think this distinction is important and separate, or are the mass shootings that have come to be prevalent in the American imagination – Columbine, Newtown, etc. related to what happens in poor (black and brown) neighborhoods?

MW: That is quite a nuanced discussion, and I am not sure that we could arrive at a definitive conclusion. Rather than get into the details, we can say that the motivation may be different, but the access to guns, the gun culture, and the ripple effects on a family and community are the same.

The nuance arrives in the motivation, and motivation is so complex that it may not be a topic we can even broach. In other words, if we can prevent the symptoms, the cause may not be worth focusing on. I think that in a generalized fashion, America cares when white college kids die, and does not care when people who society already ignores die.

KB: I was going to save this for later, but now that you've addressed it, we can go there. I saw this tweet the other day by Dan Hodges, and I thought it was particularly brilliant: "In retrospect Sandy Hook marked the end of the US gun control debate. Once America decided killing children was bearable, it was over."

I think that there is media attention when white college kids die or white kids die in general. But isn't there something to be said that after Newtown there has still been no major change to gun laws?

Those were little white children. If the deaths of little white children cannot enrage the American public enough, what will? I say this with a bitter taste in my mouth but also with the understanding of the racist society that we operate in. I'm not sure anything other than politicians willing to sacrifice their places in politics and their legacies will really change the laws. Thoughts?

MW: I do not know who Dan Hodges is, so I do not have full context, but I am not so sure that tweet is factual. If you talk to most people, they did want reform after Sandy Hook, and reform is why we are talking now.

The assumption that I think leads to this false logic is that what America wants is actually represented by the legislators and politicians in general. It seems as though everywhere you turn, problems in America are tied to politicians serving the desires of corporate donors and not the American public. I just do not believe that America accepts children dying in schools, I believe that politicians do.

KB: I think it's fair and true to say that some Americans, maybe even many Americans, want reform. But I also think that there are those who simply accept – from the politicians to the people – that "these things happen." Some see it as a negative consequence but an acceptable one in order to have the freedoms guaranteed in the Second Amendment.

And speaking of the Second Amendment, do you think it should be applied in the way it is currently? One of my personal gripes with it is there is no way that our current technology could have been foreseen at that time it was written. And because of that, does it make logical sense to apply it to the current cultural and technological environment? Are these individual liberties in this specific context that may have terrible consequences, more important than the common good? I ask knowing these things aren't mutually exclusive.

MW: I still do not know, Kovie. I observe that there is a staggering level of willful ignorance in American society. If you get people into a room and go over the facts and explain the logic, you have to be crazy not to see that what we are doing does not work, right?

Eighty million people in nearly half of the households own approximately 300 million firearms, including 100 million handguns. Two-thirds of homicides are committed with firearms. A Harvard study found that of 26 developed countries, the U.S. has 15 times the average in homicides. The frequency of mass shootings is dramatic and we have an epidemic of police shootings (or more likely a revelation of a hidden epidemic). I do not think that, if the pros and cons are honestly presented,you can leave thinking this is an acceptable consequence.

Throughout most of my life, the conservative influence of the right to bear arms made sense to me. I do not see it that way any longer. It was a slow progression for many reasons, but the one final reason was quite simple. I realized that I have carried a gun for the last 13 or so years because of the fear that someone else may be carrying one. Then, on top of that, I was carrying, and continue to, because America's answer to anyone being able to wield such a powerful weapon is that I, or someone like me, kills them before they kill you. Oh America, that cannot be the answer.

The Framers understood that things would change and built in the mechanism for amendments. There is no way that the technology and reality of today was what the Framers meant in the Second Amendment. I'm not even sure that we would come up with it today because we would not even think of it.

To anyone out there, let me tell you this: The idea that the women and men of the United States Marine Corps would conduct an amphibious landing in the harbor of Baltimore to take over the city and control the citizens is insanity. These are our friends, family, and neighbors. Technology has connected us all.

KB: You've touched on one of the myths of gun control – which is this idea that the government is going to "come and take your guns." To be perfectly honest, I find it rather childish and laughable. The reality of technology is if the government wanted to annihilate all of us, it could do so in a heartbeat. It's scary, but it's the truth.

What other gun myths do you think are prevalent among many people who don't think gun ownership should be more strictly regulated? And for that matter, what solutions do you think our culture most readily needs as far as gun laws are concerned?

MW: Of course the government could inflict serious damage by pressing buttons. And the basic idea is that a bunch of amateurs would be able to defeat the most powerful military the world has ever seen? On the flip side, the rate of gun ownership probably would make it impossible for ground forces to overtake country. But remember, they have to get through the most powerful military the world has ever seen first. That myth is about the only thing that is remotely factual. So the question for that is: how many children with bullets in their bodies are worth the fears you have?

Another myth is that people under such stress are even capable of reacting properly – that good guys with guns can and do stop bad guys with guns regularly. That more guns equals safety. Think about that for a second; it is like fighting fire with fire. It just is not logical.

For any of the myths out there, I just ask that people carry them out to their fullest and see if that makes sense. For example, a violence-free society would look like what? An armed society, with more guns, more concealed, more of the most uncontrollable variable (the human being), what does that society look like? Why in the heck is anyone working towards the society of every person being a deadly threat?

Solution-wise, I think it is very difficult to deal with the amount of guns already out there. Ideally, I would allow shotguns, incredibly strict requirements for handguns, ban all other gun type manufacturing for private sale, and continually push the facts and evidence with an education campaign to attempt to alleviate fears, and seek destruction of handguns and rifles.

KB: One of the more pervasive of ideologies that seems to prohibit any solutions, including education, not to mention legal avenues, is this notion that some Americans believe and sometimes provide bad research to support a position that "gun laws don't work."

It doesn't matter how many other comparable societies that have changed their gun laws after ONE mass shooting. Nor does it matter that the evidence to support that less homicides take place with stricter gun laws and certainly less mass shootings. Still, people, and that includes educated people will say, "gun laws don't work." What do you say that? How do you get around that?

MW: Well, I agree that gun laws do not work when the laws are on the people. What I mean by that is that it appears as though human beings cannot safely coexist with such high levels of gun saturation and a dog-eat-dog culture.

I do not have the concept fully thought out, but understand that cops are out there shooting people at an internationally alarming rate in America because they are afraid everyone has guns. They are not following the laws about pulling that trigger because of the availability of guns.

The blood of prohibition, both alcohol and other drugs, is spilled on our streets and lives are destroyed so often and easily because the gun is available. With this current reality, laws and incarceration are not the solutions. People need to understand what we are creating, apply laws against new manufacturing, and start a cultural shift that recognizes how such power corrupts.

KB: Finally, there's a part of me that has hope – because that's the right thing to do. But I also believe an individual and communities have to get to work in order for hope to be made possible and achievable.

It's one thing to talk about change, and it's another to make it happen. Of course change starts with a voice, but it doesn't end there. I have this bad feeling that even after what happened in Oregon, it won't be too long until we're having another "thoughts and prayers" session in the country over the same thing.

How do people who want change go about enacting it, both politically and within their communities?

MW: For better or for worse in how the public will take this, but thoughts and prayers do not work. We have to act. There are many of us that are acting right now and I really believe we will win. It will take time but what we are talking about are human beings winning in a just society with safe streets. With the availability of information and the work being done on the streets, we will win.

For the public that wants the future that I speak of, step 1: join and support Wolf PAC to get a Constitutional Amendment getting money out of politics so our politicians actually represent us. Step 2: Protest with us, fight for change, force the government to act on reform. If you like my message, get me or someone like me in charge.

My ultimate desire is have a federal position enacting reform – make them do that. Make your politicians put qualified leaders with these visions in charge of your police departments. I would drop my path and go to a Cincinnati (or elsewhere) to prove that we can do this, and I am far from alone. If you are a citizen, do you not want to live in fear of going to the movies or having a cop overreact to fear? If you are a cop, do you not want to work where you do not have to be afraid that every car stop contains a hidden gun? We must change our culture.

10

A Student Loan Crisis, Underpaid Adjuncts, And Dysfunctional Dialogues: What Is The Future Of Higher Education?

In August 2015, USA TODAY published an article asserting that the student loan crisis is America's next big crisis. Then there is the financial reality that adjunct professors face – a bleak narrative about inadequate compensation. And largely due to the protests in Mizzou and Yale in early November 2015, the public has asked questions regarding dialogue and debate in academic institutions where different spaces – intellectual, public, and "safe" – intersect. To get to the heart of these matters, in late November 2015, I invited Dr. Paula Young Lee, a faculty fellow at Tufts, and a columnist for Salon, to dialogue.

Kovie Biakolo: Hi, Paula, could you introduce yourself briefly and tell us about your writing and your academic background?

Paula Young Lee: Hi, Kovie! I hold a doctorate from the University of Chicago where my interdisciplinary dissertation focused on the foundations of the modern institutional sciences and their expression through architectural forms (1650-1850). I have also published widely on the architectural form of animal captivity, i.e. slaughterhouses, zoos, and farms. What I basically do is think about the ways in which the lived environment shapes and organizes everyday thought and collective values. As a fiction writer, I am currently exploring the intersection of science fact and social forms and coming up with…horror.

KB: That sounds absolutely brilliant, and I think we might need to have you write something in-depth for us regarding that knowledge-base. However, I want to move on to the subject matters of this dialogue.

The reality, I think, is that college is, practically speaking, unaffordable for a lot of people. Then there is the student loan bubble that many people are caught in. From my perspective, I think that it's pretty much unsustainable to carry on the way many universities are carrying on with students taking on huge amounts of debt to go to school. What are the effects of this on the university, and what are some potential resolutions? And without potential resolutions, what do you think the eventual outcome will be?

PYL: To answer this fully would require a few hundred pages. But in brief: many studies have commented on the "corporatization" of the university. What this means, in essence, is that the entire system shifts the end goal from education per se, to producing more consumers.

One of the ways that this can be seen is in the cost of the textbook which can be understood as a small part that represents the workings of the whole. For example, many core textbooks for required classes in math or economics will cost, say, $100.00. For working class kids who may be on scholarship, this is too expensive. They cannot afford to buy this book because each semester demands the purchase of dozens of books.

Why can't these books be borrowed from the library? Because each year a new revised version gets issued theoretically rendering the previous edition obsolete. But this is not true; it is a way to profit from the sale of books. What is going on is the exploitation of students in the name of "education," and students – and often faculty – are stuck.

The rhetoric of progressivism, of progress, and "improvement" is co-opted to serve the goals of capitalism. So what do you do? You can't pass the class unless you have the book to read, and if you have last year's edition the pages won't match the assignments, etc. So part of what is also going on is a back-handed way of preserving classed-based economic privilege while claiming that "every opportunity" is being extended to economically disadvantaged students.

I think this helps clarify the difference between obtaining *knowledge* which is written in those textbook pages, and *passing a class*, which has a lot to do with being able to buy that expensive book. That model can be extrapolated to the entire university experience. What this boils down to is the rather unsavory truth: yes, the university continues to perpetuate and reward a class that is privileged based on economic stratifications. College is indeed too expensive for most families today, and it's become impossible to work your way through thanks to exorbitant raises in tuition.

KB: I think that takes care of any follow-up questions regarding that process in particular of how economic imbalances and inequalities in the university take effect, but one thing that certainly is associated with this imbalance is the underpayment of adjuncts in the university.

So you have an institution in which only those who can really afford the pricey textbooks and the ever-increasing room and board, etc. – not to mention tuition – can be successful in the environment. But with all this money, it has almost become a public outcry, albeit one that falls on deaf ears, of adjunct professors and even associate professors being in economically devastating situations.

Is this a separate issue from the financial inequalities of merely attending school, or are they related and ultimately having to do with the university's financial replication of capitalism in its processes? Feel free to expand on what the myths and the facts are about adjuncts and associate professors and financial compensation.

PYL: These issues, including that of the student protests and the hand-wringing over "p.c. culture" are all linked. The rise of the "precariat" in all levels and segments of the working world is an apt way to understand why the institution of higher learning is under siege. But inside the university, the rise of the precariat is also an expression of a particular and stubborn strain of anti-intellectualism that has taken hold even more perniciously, as of late.

I think the stats are that 70 percent of the faculty across the board are now adjuncts. What that means is that the faculty don't have prep time, don't have support (like an office or anyone to help set up the classroom), and are often teaching on multiple campuses. When I was a student, I had no clue about the differences among different faculty ranks or their employment status; I took classes based on my schedule and my interests. I'm a nerd. I love to learn new things, and I am permanently curious about everything.

But this comes back to why one attends university in the first place. Are you there because your parents made you? Are you hoping to get a minimum degree required for a certain kind of job? Are you there because you have no other idea what to do with your life? In other words, college has newly become less about learning and more about being culturally coded as a certain kind of individual, namely, bourgeois or aspirationally bourgeois, which is why parents will take out massive loans so their children can attend classes they can't remember.

Meanwhile, for the persistent idealists among us, the college experience is supposed to be about imparting skills in critical thinking which has nothing to do with parroting information or rote memorization or terrific skills at googling. Critical thinking is the goal of all education, really. Dismantle that as the goal and poof! you've got a docile citizenry. So what we – collectively speaking, the US as a whole – have to look at is the value, or lack thereof, placed on being an educated person for its own sake – as opposed to being an educated person who therefore earns this much money because of a professional degree.

I sometimes think of the book *True Grit* where the particular dialect is a function of the historically accurate use of large words; the frontier Americans depicted were all trying very hard to improve themselves through book learning which included, but was not limited to, the Bible. There doesn't seem to be much of that intense desire to improve oneself as a cultural good, though certainly there are isolated instances.

Another way to look at it is in the depressing decline in literacy levels over the past 20 years and the fact that most adults never crack open a book to read for pleasure after they graduate from high school. Hmm. This response was kind of long-winded!

The short version is this: if you take away the capacity of faculty to focus on their students by constantly threatening to pull out the rug from under their feet, i.e. fire them or just not re-hire them (which is the usual case for contingency faculty), then the faculty have no ability to challenge their students who are now "customers" or "clients" and therefore participating in a transactional model where it is understood that you are paying for your education, which is to say, your degree. And education has little or nothing to do with it; your teacher might as well be that fast-food worker behind the counter, because the conditions of work are more or less the same.

KB: I definitely have been discouraged in my own cultural observation of what is going on in the higher education institutions with regard to the increasing customer-service relationship between students and teachers. Of course there is a place for adjuncts and there is a place for full-time professors, but what do you think that place should be?

I think what people want to know – including people who are in academic circles – is where exactly is the money going? If the cost of education is higher while the cost of hiring staff is lower then there is a discrepancy going on here, and one that isn't benefiting students or professors. So who exactly is benefiting from this model in higher education?

PYL: The institution benefits insofar as it is rewarding itself. The funding resources are going to pay for football teams, new buildings, and overall administrative costs, all of which are more outward directed towards selling an image rather than towards the unsexy task of teaching students.

Many studies have pointed to the rise of an administrative class inside the university, a class that exists to supervise and direct the flow of power inside the institution while rewarding itself. I tell everyone to read Mary Douglas's book, *How Institutions Think*, a classic analysis of institutional forms that has yet to be surpassed. Another one to read, slightly more accessible because it's a novel, is Herman Hesse's *Magister Ludi* or the *Glass Bead Game*. The basic point is that all institutions are conservative which is why I think it's so funny when I hear so much yelling about "snooty Ivy League liberals."

Individuals may hold liberal ideals, but the institution is quite the opposite. The older and the more prestigious, the more conservative it is in actual operational principles. That's how they survive over time. There are actors, and then there are agents. The true power always resides in who gets to shape the frame. You don't even see it and yet it defines everything taking place inside.

As for the place of adjuncts versus full-time professors: It used to be the case that adjuncts would teach a speciality class for which there was sporadic demand, such as pre-modern English lit or, say, a language class in Korean. Depending on the program, these adjuncts might teach regularly but only one seminar a year, and it was understood that this was supplemental to a regular full time job either as a professor elsewhere or not in academia at all.

But when you are trained to be a researcher in pre-modern English literature and dream of training others to love Boethius, then it is what you want to do with your life, wherefore you start to adjunct in hopes of securing a full time position as a regular member of the faculty. But if those positions are not there or anywhere because tenure lines are being cut, then that turns into the nightmare of being a worker-for-hire with a giant student loan and no professional future which is what too many Ph.Ds are now staring at.

KB: Taking the conversation away from the interactions between actors and agents in the higher education system, let's talk about what is going on at Yale, Mizzou, and other universities across the nation. It's interesting that you discussed earlier the conservatism of higher education. I don't think a lot of people realize this – and it's something that, if you're a person of color in a university setting especially as faculty or staff, people often think that it's a liberal space that affords people of color more opportunities and less discrimination.

I often tell people that it is a matter of asking the question "in comparison to what?" because the university setting itself is prejudiced and filled with the same institutional problems as elsewhere. Now all the same, I have written about the incidents that took place in the university with regard to how all people interact in public, intellectual, and safe spaces – and the contradictions that occur when you are a person of color in such a space.

Fundamentally, I still deem that the necessity of dialogue and diversity of thought in the university setting is of importance – for not only freedom and rights, but for the betterment of the learning process in which I tend to be on the side of bell hooks who believes that the classroom is a contested space. Nonetheless, what is your topic on this "liberalization" of academia, of how people of color operate within those settings, and how our interests as students and faculty should be approached while still maintaining the institution as a place of plurality of perspective and ideas?

PYL: The university is a utopian space, at least in theory.

Therefore it represents the no-place, the ivory tower of the fable, the apolitical sphere where ideas can mingle freely. The student protests are shattering this image, or so it would seem, except the institution has been slowly collapsing for a long time under its own weight.

To a certain extent, what is happening at Mizzou and Yale are opposite sides of the spectrum. (A public university is a different beast than a private one, and the social protocols are quite distinct.) What seems to have happened is that reality did not meet expectations. When you compete to gain admission to the Ivy League (Yale), you are perforce one of the best and the brightest and you have to fight to get access to those resources, that study time, that pressure to party instead of study. And when you choose that school, you believe you are entering into a group self-selected to be *like-minded*. Smart. Energetic. Creative. Idealistic.

What happens when the myth of meritocracy shatters? Disillusionment. Disappointment. But most of all you start to understand that utopia never existed except in your own dreams because knowledge, and the search for knowledge, is always embodied. Bodies are entities inside social space, and it doesn't matter how brilliant you are (Ta-Nahesi Coates probably articulates this better than anyone writing today): you are always inflected by, marked by, and codified by the terms of your body, by markers called "race," "gender," "age," "nationality," and so on.

So what I tend to see here, in the long view, is that finally universities are giving up Cartesian models that see mind over here and body over there and those bodies are machines made to serve, and a struggle to move it into the 21st century where we can think phenomenologically about the ways that knowledge is shaped.

People of color tend to see the working of the institutional frame and understand it as a Procrustean bed precisely because we are outside it. Marginalized voices offer up perspectives that are intrinsically critical of authority because, well, they're marginal. Michael Camille wrote a wonderful book called *Image on the Edge* about medieval marginalia, those little subversive drawings making fun of hegemonic authority by dancing and tooting on the edge of holy manuscripts. The funny part of his study is that the state of marginalization was replicated in the scholarship: for years, nobody paid any attention to those farting gargoyles or lascivious monkeys and dismissed it as being irrelevant to textual exegesis, and now they're all anyone cares about. The point is that margins and centers are spatial as well as political, and nobody ever cedes power without a fight.

KB: Finally, a short question, Paula: what is your vision for higher education in the long run? What do you think can practically be achieved, and what would you like to see stay, go, and be transformed as far as finances concerning students, compensation concerning adjuncts and professors, and the process of engagement and dialogue in the university?

PYL: Adjuncts should unionize, the student protestors are already doing a great job of acting with other student protesters on other campuses, we need tuition reform, there has to be a greater cultural respect for learning, recognizing that there is nothing to fear from different ways of thinking, and very little about the student protests is actually about p.c. culture or liberalism run amok.

It is far more about social and economic inequality that is placing enormous stress on social integrity in this country and ultimately the world. Students should stand together with faculty and lobby to get full-time faculty back into their classrooms as well as back into administrative roles. In my idealistic, fluffy way, I want students to be energized by the sheer excitement of the realm of ideas, because there is so much out there, and it can be an amazing thing to learn.

Basic excitement for researching questions is what took me around the world, and it can take anyone where they want to go. And in the students today, the capacity for excitement is still there, it's just getting crushed under the weight of competitiveness born out of fear and the demoralizing impact of ordinary cruelties. Also, I think it is important to remember that these student protesters are *students*. Franky, I am in awe.

11

We Just Can't Agree On Cultural Appropriation

Cultural appropriation is a heavily contested topic in our contemporary culture. We can't seem to agree on it, including on how to define it. Steve Patterson, an author, video producer, and "philosopher who works outside of academia" wrote an article titled "The Case for Cultural Appropriation." It was republished on Thought Catalog. In December 2015, I asked Patterson for a dialogue in order to understand, ask questions of, and challenge his assertions.

Kovie Biakolo: Hi, Steve, can you please introduce yourself? Tell us who you are, what your interests are, and what you do if you'd like.

Steve Patterson: Certainly. I am a philosopher working outside of academia. I'm interested in a lot of topics from economics and epistemology to social and political theory.

KB: First of all, having read your article, I would like to start with your definition of cultural appropriation. What is it in your own words?

SP: Depending on who you ask, you'll get different answers. So I can't say this is the "objective definition," but my article considers cultural appropriation as "acting in accordance with a different culture than the one you were born into." That could include wearing a different culture's hairstyle, listening to a different culture's music, using their language, etc.

KB: My response to that in the first place is that you're right in saying that definitions may be dynamic or as you put it, "not objective," per se. But I do think some definitions might be more comprehensive than others. For example, the definition of cultural appropriation as the mere use of an element of a different culture, or the mimicry of a different culture, is too simplistic to get to the heart of the social consequences that occur, and have the potential to occur, when cultural appropriation takes place.

I think a better definition would include taking into context the elements of power that occur when appropriation takes place. Simply borrowing features of culture can be mere cultural exchange. But cultural appropriation, I think, involves the use of elements of a culture outside of an individual's own culture such that a power imbalance occurs in how the feature is perceived by more powerful and less powerful cultures alike. Power here is used to indicate economic and socio-cultural influence which admittedly some cultures have over others. In this context, do you believe that cultural appropriation, as you assert in your article, is never wrong?

SP: Unfortunately, the more nuanced perspective on cultural appropriation has been lost in the mainstream. A recent example in Ottawa, Canada is where a university shut down a yoga class that was being taught by a white woman because of supposed "cultural appropriation." There are numerous examples of this kind of nonsense – where people of "wrong skin colors" are prescribed a certain list of approved behaviors – and that's what my article argues against.

To your point, I can see the reasoning behind being aware of context and socio-economic history, but I'm still leery of group labeling. I consider the most accurate philosophic perspective to be a kind of radical individualism where all humans are fundamentally individuals and their "group membership" is ultimately periphery.

I recognize that my skin color, for example, has shaped my experiences in the world, but it's not something essential to who I am. Therefore, I don't think it should determine what behavior I'm allowed to engage in. That doesn't give me permission to be entirely unaware and insensitive to historical cultural issues, but it does give me the responsibility and permission to act as I choose, regardless of any labels put on me.

KB: In your example of yoga, I will say that I heard of that story in Ottawa and it did tickle me quite a bit. In the first place, I don't think that's a particularly *general* or *common* example of someone claiming appropriation because the context of yoga is such that it has transformed in different cultures into different things, including a form of exercise in Western cultures. It is not necessarily a spiritual experience in the way it might have originally been practiced. However, even in that case, I would not be opposed to hearing an argument that questions its practice in Western spaces because I think when you're coming from a position of power, it is very easy to laugh and scoff at the concerns of people in cultural positions where their power is *relatively* less. Of course, this example in particular is so loaded with global dynamics that it probably deserves an entire study of its own. That said, I did find that example unhelpful in showcasing cultural appropriation as something harmful. But again, context is key.

To your assertion of skin color as an example, is it fair to say that you don't think of your skin color as intrinsic to who you are, because you're white, and therefore in this country and culture (and world) you are in a dominant social position? Part of being in a position of social dominance is that you often don't have to think about that identity. The same cannot be said for people of color, and as a black, African woman I understand that contextual difference. In African countries, I don't think about my blackness, but rather, my ethnicity. But in the West, my blackness is not dominant, and therefore, like it or not, it plays a role in my experiences – how I am perceived and how I am treated. But I don't want to make this conversation in its entirety about race.

I do want to address, too, that you might also be likely to adopt radical individualism because you're already from a culture that is individualistic relative to, for example, those who might be in subcultures in the United States or globally who come from collectivist cultures. What I'm essentially saying is that culture is so important in perspective that it is ultimately the framework many of us use to see the world, to determine our values, etc.

But it is also true that when you're from a dominant culture (the United States) and in a dominant position in that culture (white and male) that the cultural features that you participate in from other cultures has a different consequence for you than for other people – even for people who participate in their own culture. This is to say, that one of the things I think a lot of people miss about cultural appropriation is not that it is "wrong" for someone of a certain skin color or culture to participate in other cultures, it is often that those who are from less dominant cultures face prejudice and sometimes effective discrimination within a larger culture for doing so. Does that make sense?

SP: There are a lot of good points here, but I want to focus on one. You have implied a couple of times that my beliefs are a function of my skin color or group identity. This is precisely what I argue against in my article. I call it an "abstraction error." I think you're viewing the group label first then the individual second. My individualism is not a function of the culture in which I was raised – my beliefs are far more radical. For example, in stereotypical "white male culture," nationalistic pride is a big deal. In my case, "being *American*" is an essential identity. I reject this label, too. I am an individual who happens to have been born in a particular geographic area – just like I happen to be born with white skin. Both of these things affect my experience of the world, but they are not essential to my person.

You have said, and correct me if I'm mistaken, that your self-identity is as a "black, African woman." I also view this as a philosophic error, and it unnecessarily divides you and me. I see you fundamentally as an individual with black skin and African heritage. This conversation isn't between "a white, Irish man" and "a black, African woman." I see it as a conversation between two individuals who happen to have differences – and they aren't even responsible for having those differences. Neither of us chose the groups that we were born into.

I also think it demeans the individual, to a degree, by thinking his or her beliefs are only a function of their social environment. My peers – and you might say "white culture" in general – are wrong on a whole host of issues, from my perspective, and I don't think it's fair at all to lump me in with them. My beliefs, and your beliefs, are fundamentally chosen by us as individuals.

Not only do I think this is a more accurate way of seeing the world, I also think it fosters a greater degree of sympathy between individuals. I recognize that black humans in the United States face outrageous – infuriating – discrimination in the justice system especially. But I don't feel like, "Oh, isn't that a shame it's happening to 'black people.'" I think, "Damn the unjust police and court system that unfairly targets my fellow humans – my peers and equals – who have black skin!"

This doesn't mean I am unaware of imbalances of power in societies. Instead, it allows me to sympathize with any individuals who are in the unfortunate position of being less powerful, due to no other reason than their skin color or ethnicity. My sympathy, however, does not need to be coupled with restricting my behaviors because of a fear of cultural appropriation. When you look at the world through an individualist lens, "having a list of approved behavior based on group identity" just doesn't make sense.

KB: I'll start by saying with no malice but with the perspective of multiculturalism that determining how someone identifies him/herself as a "philosophical error" is exactly a form of cultural condescension coming from a global perspective in which you and I might live in the same world, but we do not encounter the same reality.

Moreover, I think while we can argue all day about whether the individual is in the primary position or the culture he or she stems from is the primary – it is a chicken and egg situation. I cannot scientifically prove that culture is more important or the individual is more important, but there is an argument for how they are both intrinsic to perspective.

I think that what you say about identification would be accurate in a world where identities are not unequally treated, or socially located in dominance and disadvantage, but that is simply not the world where we live in – where our identities have *real consequences*. And people self-identify as particular cultures not from philosophical errors as you say, but to associate heritage, to assert particular experiences with others and identify with those experiences, and also as a form of resistance because the truth of the matter is I simply cannot live my life in America as an "individual."

I am a black, African woman and that does have real consequences in this society everywhere from legally to socially and politically, and even potentially economically. This isn't a matter of opinion – it is an observable fact that can be scientifically measured in society. And again, I think that your perspective on individualism may be a function of your individual thought, but individuals don't live in a vacuum – they are influenced by their environment, culture being one of them.

That aside, I want to address the notion in your article that people's labels are divisive. This exists, I argue, because of power and dominance of some cultures over others. In a perfect world, this wouldn't have to exist because difference would be seen as a good thing rather than a bad thing. Is it not more practical to accept that people wish to be different and wish to identify as different from each other, and that should be acceptable? (This difference doesn't negate the fundamental equality of each human individual, mind you.) Indeed, I don't take the relativist view that all things in all cultures are acceptable. I take the post-positivist view that some things are objective across cultures or at least they ought to be. But when those human rights are fulfilled (which can be contested, by the way), then differences should be allowed to exist and be celebrated, rather than be dominated by one group over another.

SP: "Cultural condescension" only exists once you accept the debatable premises of "group label first, individual second." I reject this idea – not because my culture rejects it, but because I, as an individual do. I would be so bold as to say, "There is no such thing as cultural condescension! Only individuals can condescend to one another," which I am certainly not trying to do.

Also, another wonderful philosophic topic: you say "you and I might live in the same world, but we do not encounter the same reality." I couldn't disagree more strongly, and perhaps this is one of the underlying premises we disagree on. Reality is, by its definition, something objective and external. Our experiences of reality might be different, but reality remains the same. For example, somebody born with a neurological disease will have a very different experience than somebody born healthy, but that doesn't mean reality is different. They are still two individuals who happen to have arbitrary, unchosen differences between them who are experiencing the same world from different angles. Implying that "reality is different between two people" creates an uncrossable divide between them, and I don't think this is true.

One more note on this point: you say you "cannot live in America as an individual." Again, I must disagree. Not only can you live as an individual, you *are living* as an individual. Groups are not something that can act; they cannot live. Groups are simply abstractions – they are conceptual, not physical. Now, as an individual, you might closely identify with other individuals, and you might choose to strongly unify your behavior. A lot of individuals, for example, can choose to march on Washington. But it's not "a group marching on Washington" – it's "a lot of individuals *that we label as a group* marching on Washington." This might seem like a minor point, but the idea has big implications.

In regards to labels, I do agree with you that they exist largely because of differences – and imbalances of power – between people. There's a reason that most people don't strongly self-identify with their eye color; it's because eye-color is usually not associated with political or ethnic power. It's not nearly as relevant to people's experiences of reality, you might say.

I also agree that in a perfect world, labels would be entirely arbitrary (as the amount of freckles on your arm, or the size of your kneecaps – totally irrelevant). I certainly don't want to imply that labels aren't powerful, or even useful at times. But I do believe that if we want to reduce the power of labels in society, we can start immediately by seeing each other as individuals. Let other people label us and make abstraction errors – you and I, and anybody else, can see the world clearly and reject the artificial categories into which people place us.

It's like any other set of ideas. Lots of people have really nasty and destructive political ideas. That doesn't mean A) we can't have more accurate political ideas, or B) we have to "go along with" their ideas. So just because labels are powerful and pervasive in our society doesn't mean we can't see through them in the present.

Another benefit of this way of thinking: you can expose people to radical individualism who might never have encountered it. I have relatives who are only surrounded by racism and abstraction errors. They might not even know there's another way of thinking. By promoting this kind of radical human equality and identity, I think more people will become persuaded by it, getting us one step closer to a post-labeling society.

KB: We can have a debate about the philosophy of reality later, but my use of it in this context is to inform a simple observable fact of living in this country in any given space: when you are a white, American male walking into anywhere, you are labeled and perceived and ascribed to certain characteristics and privileges. Those things will be different for me as a black, African woman. Even without considering the vantage point and context, the "reality" of our experiences will be different. And especially with privilege, one of the functions of privilege is that you can't accept or deny it – it simply exists in cultural spaces because of history and power.

There are simply some experiences that you and I will not "share" because of our differences. I will never know what it's like to have the privilege of whiteness – or be able to do the destruction it does. Neither my class nor my education level makes that possible. My class or education might make it possible for me to have some privileges in society as well as do some damage. But you will not share all the experiences of what it is like to be a black woman in this country either. I don't even share all of it because of my nationality – which makes a measurable difference. These are some basic things that are supported by data collection, and showcasing patterns of groups in terms of social experiences, from the workplace, to how you and I will get perceived walking into an expensive clothing store, to just about any possible space where human interaction occurs. One can understand, one can empathize, but that does not mean one can partake in all experiences of another group of people.

To the point about me being an individual, that is rather archaic to the understanding of how lived experiences operate. I may have my own individual thoughts and actions and experiences, and they may be different from everyone else in the entire country, and in the world for that matter, but there are things that I will share with other black women and other black people and other African people and other African women that are similar. Denying this is not only a denial of a lived experience, it is potentially dangerous for safety and survival of some people whose primary identities exist in disadvantage bodies.

Groups are abstractions, sure. As is race and nationality, and arguably gender, and many other identities. I am not arguing that these things exist in nature – that is not what cultural scholars determine. Rather, what we know is that despite the social construction of these things, the consequences of these constructions are not an abstraction – they are real, identifiable, measurable things; they exist in the real world with *social consequences*. I think the notion of radical individualism is one that is simply not pragmatic in the world's current state of affairs. I would argue too that for many cultures, it is not desirable as long as inequality is a reality of their lived experiences, as a group, and as individuals.

However, philosophical exchange aside, I want to wrap this up, and finally ask: in your opinion, is there *ever* any harm done in cultural appropriation or is it always just acceptable "to borrow" without consideration of context and power and consequence? My position is not that individuals shouldn't borrow, but rather, when entire cultures face discrimination and social displacement and distortion because of another culture's (not individual's) systematic exchange, then we have to reconsider how cultures engage in this exchange.

SP: You keep wanting to divide us! I agree that our experiences are different, entirely as a function of our skin colors and the environment in which we find ourselves. It's true that my experience shopping is different from yours. I would have to be a fool to deny this. But it's not *essential* to who we are as humans or how we can relate to each other. We have lots of differences which change how we experience the world. I am 6'4 with a bad back. I assure you, in nearly every circumstance in which I find myself, the construction of my skeletal system affects my experience in a negative way. But that's not *essential* to my person. Can other "tall people with bad backs" relate my experience more than "shorter limber people?" Certainly, but that doesn't mean I am a different kind of human.

(Of course, I am not saying "height changes my daily experience as much as skin color," but the point is to say there are many, many differences between us that do not change our mutual identity as humans.)

To answer your question about appropriation, I do not believe "cultures" can exchange anything separate from individuals. Can individuals act in a way which is callous and ignorant of history? Certainly. Say somebody is a fan of the swastika as a religious symbol – it's arguably the oldest in existence. That person, even if they have the best of intentions, should be aware of the history of that symbol and the connotations made when wearing it. But that's not because "he's in the wrong ethnic group to be wearing a swastika." It's not about appropriation at all. It's because certain symbols are associated with ideas, and most people don't want to be associated with the ideas conveyed by a swastika.

So I suppose my answer is "There is no 'cultural appropriation' that is separate from the actions of individuals." I am not responsible for the behavior of other individuals who have white skin, and they aren't responsible for mine. If individuals with white skin have abused positions of authority, historically or in the present, then that's awful and condemnable. But I am not liable for it nor do I think my behavior should be suppressed because of it.

12

What Do Young Adults Think Of Donald Trump? A Conversation Between A Donald Trump Supporter And Critic

Donald Trump has been at the center of cultural conversations and debate since his latest emergence into politics. As I write this in March 2016, he is a frontrunner for the Republican nominee for president, and it looks like he may win. I suppose it is only fitting that the last dialogue in this collection is about Trump, who personifies a certain lack of civility in our civil discourse, the divisiveness it often accompanies, and the disillusionment with the status quo of politics and society, that many groups encounter(ed) in the public space prior to Trump's emergence and popularity or notoriety – depending on how you perceive him.

In a private online community for Thought Catalog writers and contributors in late January, a conversation about Donald Trump looked like it might head south quickly. Part of my role at Thought Catalog was to turn contention into productive conversation. Two writers, one who supports Trump (Jeremy Ely), and the other who is anti-Trump (Shaun Scott), agreed to engage in respectful exchange. I facilitated the experience. In many ways, it was a reminder of the possibility of civil dialogue, even in the midst of the culture wars.

———

Kovie Biakolo: *Hi all. Firstly, can you tell us a little about yourselves? Secondly, in a few sentences, can you sum up your views on Donald Trump?*

Shaun Scott: I'm a Seattle-based writer and filmmaker. I wrote a book for Thought Catalog in 2015 called *Something Better: Millennials and Late Capitalism at the Movies*. I'm currently working on a book called *Millennials and the Moments that Made US: A Cultural History of the U.S. from 1984-present*. I think Donald Trump is a savvy marketer who is not above using racist demagoguery to exacerbate class divisions and bolster his (non-existent) credentials to be President of the United States.

Jeremy Ely: I live in Los Angeles and like to write short stories and have political conversations. I don't really align to the left or to the right (for example, I think Bernie Sanders is awesome), but I also think Donald Trump presents great ideas and that he'd be a great leader for the country. I think the tremendous hatred I see toward him is a little over the top, and his ideas are not as extreme as we make them out to be.

KB: *Trump has been called a racist, sexist, and a whole host of other "ists." Do you believe that he is, and why or why not?*

JE: I don't find the terms "racist" or "sexist" that powerful anymore because of how loosely people in our generation will toss these labels on things they don't like. Prior to the Civil Rights Movement, we saw awful racism in this country. Before women could vote, we saw genuine sexism. Now we have a black president and incredible gender equality. Of course, it is not 100% equal because men are not women and women are not men. There will never be a pure absolute lack of racism and an absolute lack of gender inequality. The things Trump says, meanwhile, are not actually racist. They're just opinions that are not considered politically correct because of the hypersensitive age we live in.

SS: Donald Trump's credentials as a racist, a classist, and a xenophobe extend far beyond what he says; we should also pay attention to his actions. He was sued by no less than the Department of Justice for discriminatory practices in real estate. His words have led directly to violence against immigrants and people of color. He has argued that the wages of members of the middle class are "too high." As loud as he is, his actions actually speak louder than his words.

KB: *What, in your own words, does it mean to support Donald Trump, given his positioning by different groups as different things? As one of you is pro-Trump and the other is anti-Trump, what questions do you have of each other?*

SS: Jeremy will have to answer how he feels about supporting a candidate who thinks his wages are too high and who makes inflammatory statements about immigrants in public while hiring them in private.

JE: I think it's refreshing to have a presidential candidate who fearlessly states his beliefs and doesn't buy into the generic "mumbo jumbo" that most politicians preach. Again, I don't think his comments against illegal immigrants classify as racist. Part of the reason American Health Care is such a mess, for example, is because so many people are pouring into this country and it's difficult to classify who is a citizen. And, even if he were racist, he employs thousands of immigrants and gives them a living, and that's very valuable.

SS: Jeremy, what is your evidence for the claim that "health care is a mess" because of immigrants? Concrete data points in the exact opposite direction of what you say; if it weren't for the labor of immigrant communities, many in this country would go without care. And, once and for all, fearlessly stating one's belief does not, in and of itself, make one an eligible candidate to be president; if that were the case, we could elect Beavis or Butthead.

JE: European countries provide health care to all. I think people of all classes should be able to receive health care to keep living; we need to become like Europe. Poor people facing hundreds of thousands of dollars in health bills is not just, or American – all people have the right to a doctor. But if thousands of undocumented people are coming in to a country per day, it'll be impossible to institute that policy because who is an American? "The Wall" would solve that.

SS: If you want American healthcare to resemble European welfare states, I believe you should be backing Bernie Sanders. The "thousands of undocumented people" you talk about are being employed by the candidate you support; he does not have an interest in actually keeping them out, so you shouldn't either. I agree with what you say about access to healthcare being a universal right.

KB: *Moving away from immigration, how do you think Trump does on the world stage? How do you think the international community perceives Trump, and how would they perceive the United States were he to be elected? Would America be viewed as courageous or crazy, and does it matter?*

JE: Firstly, I think it does not matter very much. In life at any level, I think it's valuable to state your beliefs and not be overly concerned with other peoples' perceptions of them. Not to compare Trump to either guy, but Galileo was hated, and Hitler was loved. I'm sure people would think he's crazy, as many do in America, but that's irrelevant because I think he's right: someone needs to be courageous in the face of growing Islamic terrorism and anti-Americanism.

SS: We already know the answer to this question. Several world leaders have denounced Donald Trump, including the Prime Minister of Britain. A petition to ban Trump from traveling to England garnered 600,000 signatures. Recently, a Russian photojournalist traveling in Iowa during the caucus said that Trump reminds him of the megalomania of Putin, who is not looked on favorably in the global community. On top of that, several Pentagon staffers (and other government officials) have said they will retire if Trump wins. Trump cannot "make America great again" if his election is seen as a national embarrassment. He can't "be courageous in the face of Islamic terrorism" if he's been denounced by Benjamin Netanyahu.

JE: European countries not supporting our president aren't going to have a real effect, I don't think. They hardly do anything for us, anyway. If England wants to ban him, that's not our problem, and let's be cognizant of how Putin, the leader of another superpower, actually endorsed him, a potential American leader, which hasn't happened for decades. So I think he can get along with leaders when it matters. Trump has repeatedly said that he will make the military a priority: "I will make our military so strong, we'll never have to use it." I think that's a good state of mind.

KB: *It's a pretty big statement to say, "[European countries] do hardly anything for us anyway." Economic partnerships, political agreements, and support from the international community is important in today's increasingly globalized world as they always have been since the emergence of the nation-state. With that said, would the election of Trump see a new age of isolationism in the United States? And with trying to fight terrorism, which is a global problem, how does this affect American national security?*

SS: Here's the thing about national security interests; there are no do-overs. Trump is used to filing for bankruptcy when a business venture goes under. Businesses he's owned have done it four times. But four similar errors in judgment will result in the loss of lives. That's not a risk we can afford to take.

JE: As a man who has amassed billions of dollars of wealth working with people, I have confidence that the guy knows how to get along with people when it matters. By "poor judgment" – pissing off the British leader, or Megyn Kelly, when he's just a candidate – isn't going to result in lost lives. Out of the many businesses he's launched, it's only natural that some of them fail. Let's keep in mind that unlike Hillary Clinton, Trump spoke out against the war in Iraq in 2004, which has proven to be a disaster and a tragic loss of American and Iraqi lives and money.

SS: Actually, his lapses in judgment have resulted in violence. There was a beating of a Hispanic man in Boston that was tied to his rhetoric. The claim that he will "get along with people when it matters" implies that he has not done so thus far. If it "does not matter" during his bid to be president, it will never matter. He's unfit to lead.

JE: I think his judgment internationally trumps other candidates. In fighting ISIS, for example, Trump has repeatedly called for "taking the oil." That oil now funds ISIS. Other leaders don't have the courage to pitch an idea like this.

SS: Even a broken clock is right two times a day.

KB: *Wrapping this up, all signs point to the likelihood that Trump will not become the next president of the United States.*

But what, if anything, does it say about the country in 2016 that Trump has managed to galvanize the support he has?

JE: I hope people focus less on the occasional crazy things he says and keep in mind his rational ideas. He has called for reducing taxes for the lower and middle class, while also taxing people like himself more. I also respect his plan to help the homeless – American homelessness is shameful. I think the support he's got speaks amazingly well to the idea that people will resonate with a person who speaks their language. I think it's his unique, conversational, often humorous tone in speeches is what gets people to truly support him.

SS: All of Trump's (few) progressive ideas are available in other candidates. These other candidates do not come with the added baggage of hate speech that further divides the country and alienates world leaders. Trump represents the cultural triumph of reality television; fortunately, he will not be representing the country as an elected official.

Acknowledgements

I would like to express my immense gratitude to all who participated in these dialogues. Thank you to:

Kavita Das
Jeremy Ely
Daniel Hayes
Dr. Paula Young Lee
Dr. Logan Levkoff
Jordan Parker
Steve Patterson
Aida Rodriguez
Shaun Scott
Jeremy Sheeler
Steve Ward
Dixon D. White
Michael A. Wood Jr.

It goes without saying that without people with whom to exchange ideas, such a compilation would not exist. The hours spent on the phone, e-mail, Google Docs, etc. scheduling and planning and writing and taking time to do so in spite of busy schedules is not lost on me. Truly I am thankful.

I would also like to thank the Thought Catalog Books team, notably Chris Lavergne (TC's founder) who initially proposed the compilation, and all the TC Books staff, especially Alex Zulauf and KJ Parish. A special thanks to my friend, lifetime editor, and perpetual sounding board, Mink Choi, who originally emended and polished many of these dialogues. Further gratitude must be extended to my former professor and thesis supervisor Dr. Barbara Speicher whose guidance in my academic work greatly influences all my cultural work away from academic spaces.

I must also thank my family and friends who indulge me in private dialogues; these conversations foster the courage to engage in public discourse. Notably my brother Ejus, who fiercely challenges my viewpoints regularly, and my parents, who are also my first teachers, and whose example in academia and beyond, provide the foundation for my convictions in culture and communication. Finally, my acknowledgments would be incomplete without gratitude to God who makes all things possible.

Afterword

Upon going through these dialogues over and over again in compiling this collection, it is not lost on me that I didn't get to many important issues in the culture wars, including but not limited to abortion, marriage, religion, LGBTQIA issues, etc. It would have been my great pleasure to cover all these topics (and more) in dialogue form. However, due to many factors, including who responded to invitations to dialogue (and who did not), as well as the general constraint of time and timing, I was not always able to achieve my topical dialogue goals within the 12-month period these conversations took place.

Nonetheless, the internet is a wonderful place for organizing conversation, and I would encourage others, whether you work formally in media or not, to reproduce these dialogue formats for cultural topics of your interest. Moreover, when time allows, I am always available for a dialogue, so do not hesitate to reach me at my public writer's email address, writekovie@gmail.com, to dialogue, or for any other reason.

Sincerely,

Kovie Biakolo

Thought Catalog, it's a website.

www.thoughtcatalog.com

Social

facebook.com/thoughtcatalog
twitter.com/thoughtcatalog
tumblr.com/thoughtcatalog
instagram.com/thoughtcatalog

Corporate

www.thought.is

www.ingramcontent.com/pod-product-compliance
Lightning Source LLC
Chambersburg PA
CBHW050451290526
45786CB00006B/2250